America Bizarro

A Guide to Freaky Festivals,
Groovy Gatherings, Kooky Contests,
and Other Strange
Happenings Across the U.S.A.

America Bizarro

A Guide to Freaky Festivals,
Groovy Gatherings, Kooky Contests,
and Other Strange
Happenings Across the U.S.A.

Nelson Taylor

ST. MARTIN'S GRIFFIN
NEW YORK

Book design and some illustrations by pink design, inc., (www.pinkdesigninc.com)

Library of Congress Cataloging-in-Publication Data

Taylor, Nelson (William Nelson).
    America bizarro: a guide to freaky festivals, groovy gatherings, kooky
  contests, and other strange happenings across the U.S.A. / Nelson Taylor.—
  1st ed.
        p. cm.
  ISBN 0-312-26286-8 (pbk.)
    1. Festivals—United States—Directories. 2. Freak shows—United States—
  Directories. 3. Contests—United States—Directories. I. Title.

GT3930 .T39 2000
394.26973—dc21

00-027843

10 9 8 7 6 5 4 3 2

For Kelly, without whom I would be lost

CONTENTS

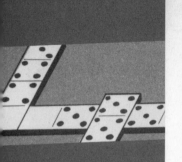

Acknowledgments

This book began as a series of articles
for *Bikini* magazine called "The Boonies."
Others have appeared, in different form,
in *Maxim*, *POV*, and *Bizarre* (UK) magazines.
I'd also like to thank the National Endowment for
the Arts for their multi-million-dollar generosity,
the entire Yaddo community for their encouragement
and support, and the 92nd Street Y for giving me
the platform to share my work with the world.
I'd also like to thank my father, who introduced me
to foot slapping, pecan shell smoking chips, and
nylon fan blade covers. Then there's my mom, who
put up with dip spit, monster trucks, and marijuana
trees. And there's my sister, who hunked so many
shoes and tennis rackets at me it was inevitable that
I become a fighter. Finally, I give a big Chevy
"hell yea!" to all the wild-eyed nameless
Americans out there who made
this book possible.

INTRODUCTION

America Bizarro is a unique travel guide that celebrates humorously interesting, pop-culture kitschy and off-the-map odd festivals; out-of-the-way gatherings; kooky conventions, conferences and contests throughout the United States. Whether the subject is music, sports, arts, food, nature, dance, the paranormal or the uncategorized strange, this is the real deal—uncensored and authentic—the one-of-a-kind who, what, when, where and how of offbeat America.

My first adventure into the oddball underbelly of America was when I covered the National Hobo Convention for *Bikini* magazine in August of 1998. When I stumbled upon the convention listing in *Chase's Calendar of Events*, I was surprised to learn that there were still hobos hopping freights, much less meeting every year to drink heavily, mourn passed brethren, discuss the state of the American hobo and elect a king and queen. I was hooked. After doing only a small amount of research, I pitched it to my editor at *Bikini*, Rob Hill. He loved it.

I did not dig too deeply into hobo culture before arriving in Britt, Iowa, the undisputed home away from the tracks for countless rail riders. I wanted to experience that world on its own terms with no preconceived notions. What I found was much more than I ever expected, a microcosm of America, a vast alterna-culture gathering of men and women who are as complex and diverse as folks in the "real" world. I met Windy City Tom, a bicycle hobo and musician from Chicago; Shadow (a recovering heroin addict) and Speedy, a hobo couple in their early twenties who sold their poems and photographs; Bandana, a part-time hobo and homosexual Catholic priest from Indiana; New York Slim, a six-foot-four-inch African-American hobo and Vietnam vet; and Steam Train Maury, a graybeard hobo who had retired from his vagabond profession. I met many others from every age bracket and variety of backgrounds, each with his or her own rough-textured reasons for living the life of a hobo.

Sitting around the campfire that was always burning at this hobo jungle, listening to the hobos share stories about scrapping metal and barely outsmarting the railroad cops (known as "bulls"), I began to realize the extent of my fascination for people living on the fringes of society—the ways that they roll and tumble and especially the ways that they celebrate their lives. So I continued my search, discovering questionable events in small hamlets like Viola, Minnesota, whose residents trap the gophers that jeopardize their crops, hack their legs off, and then save them until the annual Gopher Count, where the legs fetch a pretty price. On the lighter side I found towns like Beaver, Oklahoma, whose World Cow Chip Throwing Contest not only puts them on the national map, but brings needed revenue to a struggling economy.

Knee-deep in back-road America, I met interesting people, like L-Bow, the local color of East Dublin, Georgia, and spokesman of the Summer Redneck Games, where fat men in overalls bob for pigs' feet and their women compete for the big-hair crown. Then there's Philip Calhoun, the 1999 winner of Longview, Texas's Hands on a Hard Body Contest, who for two months after the event woke up every morning with his hands on his bed waiting for the whistle so he could pee. Or who can forget Burger Fest royalty like Violet Guaerke, the only surviving daughter of Seymour, Wisconsin's very own Charlie Nagreen, father of the American hamburger. Hearing her chant her father's sales pitch—"Hamburger, hamburger, hamburger hot, with an onion in the middle and a pickle on top, makes your lips go flippity-flop"—well, it sent chills up my spine.

As I began to regularly cover such strange events as the Pickle Fest, the Bald-is-Beautiful Convention, the Great American Bathtub Race, the Coon-Dog Graveyard Celebration, and the World's Largest Machine Gun Shoot for *Bikini* and other magazines, such as *Maxim* and *Bizarre*, which is in the United Kingdom, I realized that this world of strange happenings had never been collected into a tongue-in-cheek, reader-friendly guidebook geared toward the physical traveler and the armchair traveler alike. Let's face it, unique, authentically American experiences are growing harder and harder to find. *America Bizarro* is packed with fresh fodder for done-it-all, seen-it-all explorers.

Particular events made the cut based on my own personal criteria for what is either humorous or unique. Yet, I still had to lay down some ground rules. As one would expect, there are oodles of similar events taking place annually around the country. For instance, there are many rattlesnake round-ups, but there is only one World's Largest Rattlesnake Round-up, and that's in Sweetwater, Texas. In each category, I selected only one. Every entry falls under one of the following categories: largest, oldest or most unique. Sure, I bent the rules now and then, including events based on their humor factor alone.

Many events didn't make it into this book. Bizarre religious and racial-bashing events, such as KKK gatherings, were avoided, because I can find nothing humorous about a history rich in hate. From the get-go, I also decided that I would steer clear of Civil War reenactments, mountain men's rendezvous, Renaissance festivals and parades (for the most part), because they are each a whole world in themselves, worthy of guidebooks of their own. There are certainly many events that deserve to be included but are not because they are either too disorganized, or I did not manage to unearth them from the vast American landscape. I do feel that this book only scratches the surface of the weirdness that is actually out there, which opens the door for Part Deux in the near future. Many smaller towns don't have a voice, such as a tourism board or a chamber of commerce, and there are probably lots of events out there that a local chamber doesn't wish to promote, for whatever reasons. If you know of an event that you feel I have overlooked, please don't hesitate to write me a note. My e-mail address is included at the end of this introduction.

It goes without saying that some states are more bizarre than others. In general, and as might be expected, the West Coast is more bizarre than the rest of the country. The Top Five Most Bizarre States, in order, are Texas, California, Arkansas, Illinois and Wisconsin. I was very surprised by the latter three. Honorable mentions go to Alaska, Washington State and Colorado. Conversely, the Top Five Lamest States, in order, are Rhode Island, Idaho, New Hampshire, Vermont, and a tie for fifth place between Delaware and Iowa. Less-than-honorable mentions go to North Dakota, Oklahoma and Nebraska. These eight states have little to no sense of humor. Shame on you bad states.

Finally, I want to say that if I have offended you, your hobby, your passion or your civic pride, please accept my sincerest apology; that is not my goal. My intention is to present an informative, breezy and humorous document that views America through a kaleidoscope of colors. I believe that if we can't laugh at ourselves we will never truly understand the glory of a country filled with such a diversity of people. I hope you have as much fun with this as I had researching and writing it. Now ... welcome to *America Bizarro*.

—Nelson Taylor

Park Slope, Brooklyn
November 21, 1999
americabizarro@hotmail.com

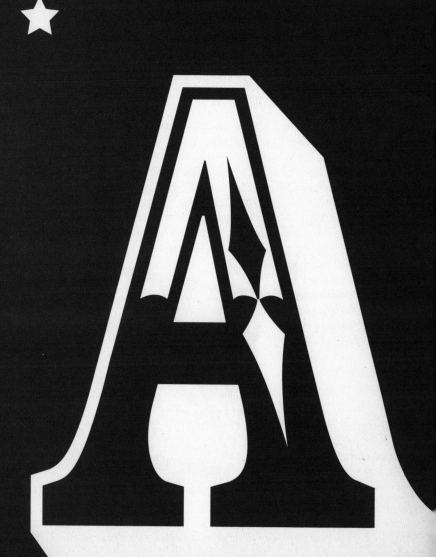

ALABAMA

World Championship Domino Tournament

For all you thrill seekers, here's one that will really put a swarm of hornets in your shorts. Dominos...say it with me "DOMINOS." For two days in early July every year since 1975, the city of Andalusia goes black-and-white wild at the World Championship Domino Tournament. We're talking men's, women's and children's competitions. And get this, they got singles and doubles, not to mention a little round-robin action. And the purse? Baby, it's big. Retirement city here I come. Almost $18,000 is given out every year, with up to $3,000 going to first-placers. And that ain't bad when you figure you only have to pay between $10 and $30 to enter. For those of you in the dark about this extreme and historic sport, here's a little trivia. Did you know the oldest domino set was discovered in the tomb of King Tutankhamen, yes, the funky Tut? Other famous domino dudes? Try President Lyndon Baines Johnson on for size! Them britches are hard to fill.

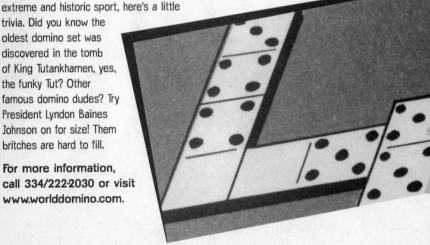

For more information, call 334/222-2030 or visit www.worlddomino.com.

World's Smallest St. Patrick's Day Parade

Can you say "one"? That's right, this is a party for one, and it has occurred every St. Patrick's Day since 1993 in the town of Enterprise, Alabama. Each year a different person of Irish descent holds the Irish flag high above head, carries a pot o' gold and recites limericks as he or she walks past the local courthouse and around the Boll Weevil Monument. (Yes, Enterprise is the only American city with a monument to a pest. Don't ask!) Grand marshals in absentia are nominated and selected on the basis of their written acceptance speech, plus their reasons for not being able to attend the parade. In other words anyone can be a grand marshal.

For an application or more info call 334/347-0581.

Coon Dog Graveyard Celebration

T his event isn't for everyone. It's only for those who are truly committed to experiencing the authentic outer edges of American life. Every Labor Day the Tennessee Valley Coon-Hunters Association (TVCHA) throws a bash at the only coon-dog graveyard in the nation. Pardon? You heard me. Since September 4, 1937, when Key Underwood buried his legendary coon dog, Troop, in the Freedom Hills Cemetery, over one hundred coon dogs have been buried here. (Nobody seems to know the exact number.) Every year coon hunters and their dogs show up—flowers in hands and mouths—to pay respects to their long-departed brethren.

What exactly is coon hunting? Well, it's a dying trade. Because there is no longer much of a demand for raccoon pelts or meat, coon hunting is now considered more of a sport than an occupation. In other words, coon hunters can't make enough cash to make a living. Now they make their money any way they can. For example, O'Neal Bolton, a born-and-bred coon killer and spokesperson for the event, tries to get money out of me for an interview. I, of course, decline his offer. In a Southern drawl so thick you could spread it on Wonder Bread, he says,

"Well, just wait a cotton pickin' minute. You going to sell this book for money ain't you?"

I nod, don't say a word.

"Oh, well, the hell with it. I'll tell you. You see, cooning is kind of like a ball game. You see if your dog gonna do it to it to his tonight or not. They race each other for the coons. You hunt with your buddies."

Now I can't get him to shut up. He goes on to tell me there's plenty of homemade wine over here, bluegrass music over there, a liars' contest right yonder, not to mention some good grub later on.

"Coon burgers?"

"No," Bolton says. "We used to have a barbecue-coon supper years ago, but this younger generation don't want to do nothing no more. Them coons eat good, though."

Be careful, the admission price is whatever they can get out of you.

For more information, call 256/332-3105.

ALASKA

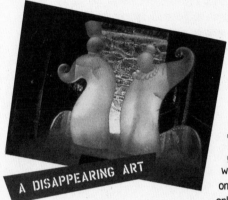

A DISAPPEARING ART

World Ice Art Championships

Every March Fairbanks is the place to be for anyone involved or interested in the world of ice carving. Sculptors can compete in one of three events—the first two by invitation only. The Single Block Classic consists of forty pairs of sculptors who each work their magic on a block of ice measuring five-by-eight-by-three feet and weighing about 7,800 pounds. Recent standouts include dragons and pirate ships. For the Multi-Block Competition, twenty teams of four each attack twelve blocks of ice measuring four-by-four-by-three feet and weighing 3,000 pounds. For this event sculptors are provided with heavy equipment to move the massive blocks of ice. Examples include a dog team with sled and native dancers joined by a dancing bear.

The final event, the Fairbanks Open, is reserved for anyone over the age of sixteen who is interested in trying their hand at ice carving. However, to be eligible, contestants must complete an ice-sculpting class. Day passes for the public are $6 for adults, $5 for seniors (fifty-five plus), $2 for children six to twelve years old; passes are free for kids under the age of five. Hint: Nighttime is the right time to view the sculptures, when colored lights bring the shimmering statues to life. As Chairman Dick Brickley likes to say, "Have an ice day!"

For more information, call 907/451-8250 or visit www.icealaska.com.

Don't miss America's original game of Human Shuffleboard, which takes place every March at the Fairbanks Winter Carnival.

For details call 907/452-1105.

Hairy Chest, Legs and Beard Contests

These annual July events are part of Fairbanks' Golden Days, a weekend that celebrates the city's rich gold-mining history, especially the late Felix Pedro, who was the first person to strike gold in Fairbanks in 1902. Since most miners were of the scraggly, unkempt persuasion, there's a Hairy Chest, Hairy Legs, Best Beard and Best Mustache contest. There's also a rubber-duck race on the Chena River. $20,000 worth of prize money is given away throughout the weekend. Warning! You better watch your p's and q's, because bad behavior can easily lead the local law enforcement to arrest your ass and toss you in the slammer.

For more information call 907/452-1105.

Wearable Art Show

AFC PHOTO

While I wouldn't advise a long-distance trek to cozy little Ketchikan for the Wearable Art Show, held every February since 1986, if you're in the area, this one's got the goods. Each year it features a new theme, such as "Living on the Edge," "Fantasy Island," or "Garbage into Gold." Area artists, housewives, bankers, butchers, you name it, spend a substantial portion of the year (especially during the long winters) in their basements creating wild, wearable works of art out of various textiles, papier-mâché, tarps, foliage and an assortment of junk. Local competition is fierce, so rumors fly all year about who was seen where talking to whom about what kind of hard-to-find material. It's got all the makings of a Flannery O'Connor story set in the Cold Country. A recent entry for the show, created by Sara Lawson, was a ball gown made almost entirely out of chicken wire. Tickets for the fashion show are $15 for adults and $10 for children, students, and seniors.

For more information, call 907/225-2211.

IT'S AMAZING WHAT YOU CAN DO WITH A LITTLE CHICKEN WIRE. POLYESTER. AND SOME OLD CDS

Pillar Mountain Golf Classic

What kind of golf tournament has rules that prohibit two-way radios, dogs, tracking devices, chainsaws and hatchets? Only one, the Pillar Mountain Golf Classic. This day-tourney, held on April Fools' Day weekend every year since 1984, offers some of the worst lies the sport has ever seen. Why? Because the course is the 1,400-foot mountain itself and the tournament is the world's only one-hole par seventy. And that isn't even the worst of it. Players are warned about extreme wind and the possibility of frostbite; they are even urged to carry a set of crampons (spiked shoes used for serious mountaineering). You see, in April Pillar Mountain often is still covered with snow and ice. But harsh conditions don't stop the sixty or so hard-core golfers who every year pay $50 to test themselves against the mountain and hopefully take home the $600 winning purse. Well, calling them golfers might be a stretch. Most are hackers who play once a year at most. Micky Mummert-Crawford, one of the female hackers who plays annually, says, "It's grueling. I shot like an eight hundred. My arms were so tired." She laughs, "I went to Hawaii last winter and played golf for the first time on a real course. It seemed so easy." If you're planning on heading to Kodiak to try your hand at guerilla golf, remember to bring lots of balls.

For more information, call 907/486-9489.

Nenana

Come to Nenana every first weekend in March for a festival that revolves around guessing the exact time of the ice breakup of Tanana River. Then head on over to the Banana-Eating Contest. No kidding.

For details call Hanna Anna Bandanna (kidding) at 907/832-5888.

Great American Bathtub Race

Northern Exposure might as well have been filmed in nowhere Nome. Once Alaska's largest city, now Nome is a five thousand-person polar speck on the map (just a stone's throw from Russia) that hasn't seen the good old days since the gold rush over one hundred years ago. But this sure doesn't keep these poor bastards from having a hell of a bash every Labor Day, when they stage the oldest bathtub race in America.

"Anybody that has a bathtub that can get it on wheels is welcome to join," says big-bellied, gray-bearded Leo Rasmussen, one of the race's founding fathers and the only citizen to have annually competed in the race for its entire twenty-two-year existence. While most racers excavate their crafts from the local dump, Rasmussen lifted his fresh from an abandoned house. He also keeps an extra tub wheeled and ready for any

LEO RASMUSSEN

THE ANNUAL BATH IS A BIG OCCASION IN NOWHERE NOME

last minute entries. Each team who enters the race (for a $20 fee) must have five members, one who rides in the tub (full of hot, bubbly water) and four who push and pull their cruiser down Front Street through the center of town.

Rasmussen's strategy is an arsenal of water balloons. But don't put your money on his slow-roller, because he rides an old iron claw-foot "that kills the horse that pulls it." In the race's history, Rasmussen's team has won only once, beating arch-rival Arctic Lighterage—"and that's because they did their training at the bar," he explains. Booze, bathing and barfing—there's nowhere like Nome.

For more information, call 907/443-2798.

ARIZONA

Egg-Frying Contest

Oatman (elevation 2,800 feet) is certainly not the hottest spot in America, but the sidewalks surrounding this 159-person town get pretty hot every July fourth—106 degrees to be precise. To celebrate their heat, Oatman hosts an annual solar egg-frying contest. In front of a crowd of about 1,500, every year about twenty contestants use anything from aluminum foil to magnifying glasses to homegrown solar devices to get an egg fried in fifteen minutes or less. Fred Eck from the Oatman Chamber of Commerce says, "There was one guy one year who even cooked potatoes and bacon with his egg." But beware, the hills around Oatman house quite a population of egg-loving wild burros. That's right, and you should expect to see a good many of them strolling the streets looking for ways to be stubborn. The contest costs nothing to enter, and winners win nothing but fifteen minutes of small-town fame. What a concept!

For more information, call 520/763-5885.

STEP RIGHT UP THE NEW HOMELESS COOKING KIT

World's Oldest Rodeo

D on't miss the World's Oldest Rodeo held every first weekend in July
since 1888.

For details call 800/358-1888.

Blooming of the World's Largest Rose Tree

E very April the town of Tombstone, home of the historic OK Corral gunfight,
celebrates the blooming of the World's Largest Rose Tree, singled out in the
thirties by Robert Ripley in his famous "Believe It or Not" column. (The idea behind
Ripley's forays into wild, weird America became a popular television show in the
eighties, hosted by Jack Palance.) The Lady Bankia rose tree, which was planted in
1885, is Guinness's undisputed world record holder. Growing bigger by the year,
the Lady Blankia hosts over a million blossoms that spread out over 8,000
square feet.

For more info call 520/457-9317.

ARKANSAS

Picklefest

If you're road-tripping through the smoldering South this May and get a flat in Nowheresville, Arkansas, you've got to hit Picklefest. Atkins, Arkansas, is Pickle City, U.S.A. No joke. This 3,400-person town eats, drinks and breathes pickles. Literally. And because the town's biggest resource is the Dean Pickle & Specialty Products Company, the pickle paves its golden road.

Speaking of dough, Atkins claims they are the inventors of the deep-fried pickle. It's one of the many street delicacies served during the fest, which has attracted some 10,000 tourists since its inception in 1992. "Now that pickle batter is a secret mixture," says Chuck Colflesh, former President of People for a Better Atkins. "If we told anyone what it was, we might have to kill them," he laughs. Chuck, who took time away from watching his afternoon rerun of the sitcom *Empty Nest*, just might be the pickle's number one fan. "I love dill pickles," Chuck says. "You can buy one just about anywhere in this town for a quarter."

It gets better. Atkins is also the home of America's only organized pickle-juice drinking contest. Can anyone say Technicolor yawn? That's right, step on up, pound a jar of nuclear green vinegar and sumptuous spices and then try to hold it down. Chuck admits that he likes pickle juice, but not that much. "No, sir. You get a few every year that turn the same color as the juice," he says. "And sometimes it comes back up."

Not like any loyal resident of Atkins could imagine such heresy, but there's just no shaking the pickle here. Their clothes have even absorbed the smell. Chuck says, "I tell you, when the factory is brewing them pickles, you can smell it for miles." This is the point in the interview where Chuck seems to get a frog (pickle?) in his throat. He pauses. Tears? You can almost hear him thinking. Then he finishes, "You know, it's a pride thing."

For more information, call 501/641-7210.

National Championship Chuckwagon Race

ach year the Tuesday before Labor Day, the small town of Clinton in the Ozark Mountains kicks off almost a week of Western competition that includes the National Championship Chuckwagon Race, the world's largest wagon race. More than one hundred three-person teams compete in front of a crowd of about 20,000, who sit along the bluffs that rise above the rangeland track. (Hint: Bring lawn chairs, a blanket, a picnic basket and a cooler.) Each racing team consists of a cook, a driver and an outrider. Chuck wagon racers compete in a series of one-on-one, high-speed battles, in which a sharp turn can send a wagon tumbling. Other weekend attractions include a six-hour Rough Riders Trail Ride, an Antique Western Auction and Mule Qualifying Trials for various asinine events. Expect lots of friendly fiddling and all-you-can-eat barbecue as well.

Held annually since 1985, the races attract mostly the same people year after year, who come to Clinton in early August to claim their favorite campsites. If you're a first-timer and plan on camping, make sure you call ahead to reserve a spot: hookups rent for $45 for the weekend. Daily admission fees are $10 for adults and $5 for children.

For more information, call 501/745-8407 or visit www.chuckwagonraces.com.

World Championship Rotary Tiller Races

Imagine tilling your garden, wishing your damn machine moved a little faster so you could soon relax under the shade of looming a elm and work on a six-pack of Bud. That's the likely origin of the World Championship Rotary Tiller Races, held every June since 1990 in the 317-person town of Emerson, Arkansas. Outfitted with tuned tillers and old ski goggles from the garage, racers fly down Emerson's 200-foot championship racetrack in search of little garden-variety glory. Well, calling the course a racetrack is probably stretching it a little. Maybe fallow field is more accurate. The annual emcee of the event, Bill Dailey, says, "We're hoping someday for a tiller racing stadium, but right now the event is just out in the middle of nowhere."

GARDENING AT 19 MPH!

BILL DAILEY

In 1998 Ronnie Hughey, a five-year veteran of the event, skippered his modified tiller into the world-record seat with a time of 7.37 seconds. How fast is that? "Faster than I am," Ronnie says. But for all you speed snobs out there, that's a whopping 18.5 miles per hour. We're talking blurrrrrrr, baby. But what's Ronnie's secret? For starters, he made his own machine with the hands the Almighty gave him. Others have spent upwards of $2,500 on professionally modified machines—alcohol-burning engines et al. But Ronnie took his 185-cubic-centimeter-capacity engine from a Honda three-wheeler, because as he so slyly deduced, the power isn't just in the punch. The Kellers (a family of racers who are Hughey's biggest rivals) have a rototiller that uses a 425-cubic-centimeter-capacity Suzuki motorcycle motor. Hughey laughs, "When he took off last year, he was digging a hole to China." Ronnie also made another smart move. He realized that since his weight would be on the back, it only made sense to put his tires on the back. Fucking genius!

Unlike most small-time competitions, the winner of the World Championship Rotary Tiller Races takes home a substantial cash price: 1,000 clams. That works out to about $8,141.11 an hour, or $135.69 a second, which is better than a good day on Wall Street.

For more information, call 870/696-3360 or visit www.purplehull.com.

Ozark UFO Conference

While this isn't the largest UFO conference in the nation, it just might be the most respected: that's because it is a completely independent event having no affiliation with any local or national UFO organization or publication. This means, if you'll excuse the pun, the sky is the limit. Handpicked authors, researchers and lecturers gather to talk about everything from abduction to electromagnetic fields to UFO healings. In 1999 speakers discussed individual cases at length, plus gave an annual report of little-known sightings and weird goings-on from around the world. Held every April since 1988, this event is open to the public for a price of $35 per head.

For more information, call 501/354-2558.

World Championship Cardboard Boat Race

Leave it to Bill Clinton's home state to perfect the art of keeping a cardboard boat from sinking. Every July since 1987 folks from around Arkansas and its environs have retreated to Greers Ferry Lake to race homemade boats—boats fashioned from cardboard, duct tape, glue and paint. "Certain sealants are okay, too," says Bill Inman of the Heber Springs Chamber of Commerce. "Just as long as it's not epoxy or fiberglass." How the hell do they stay afloat? "A lot of times they don't," Inman says. "But you have to remember that there's lots of laminated cardboard that's really quite strong." Hint: Don't forget about cardboard poster tubes, which can be used as pontoons.

Although the boats have traditionally been propelled by paddles, for the 1999 race, the board voted to allow creative propulsion devices as long as they are human-powered. Think paddleboats fueled by persistent pedaling. Seventy to one hundred boats, with crews ranging anywhere from one to eight people, cut the water through a 200-yard course. That is, as long as they don't sink first. Yet such unworthy engineers still have a shot at a prize, the Titanic Award, which is reserved for the most dramatic downing. The best craft in recent years was a 42.5-foot replica of the USS *Missouri*, which, though slow, made it across the finish line. While spectating is free, to compete in the race costs $15 per person.

For more information, call 501/362-2444.

on't miss Magnolia's World Championship Steak Cook-Off held every May. **For details call 800/482-3330.**

Bean Fest and Great Championship Outhouse Race

very October this small eclectic town hosts a weekend full of food, madness and music. About thirty two-person teams show up annually to compete in one of the world's only bean cook-offs. Although the beans, water, kettles and fire are provided by the Mountain View Chamber of Commerce, each team must provide their own secret herbs and spices. While the chefs are waiting to hear the results of the contest, the crowd sucks down over 1,000 pounds of beans and a wagon full of corn bread. Of course, nothing follows beans better than an outhouse. But these outhouses are not for doing the dirty deed. These outhouses are decorated, mounted on wheels and raced through the middle of town. The added edge of not wanting to be downwind of any racer makes the atmosphere extremely competitive. When you're not eating or farting around, you can sit down under a tree and enjoy lots of impromptu folk, gospel and country music. This event is free and attracts about 40,000 visitors.

For more information, call 870/269-8068.

Tribute to Grandpa Jones

fter the recent passing of Grandpa Jones—Country Music Hall of Fame banjo player and star of the TV series *Hee Haw*—the Ozark Folk Center decided to mount a tribute to his music and life. In September 1999, 700 people showed up to listen to family and friends of Grandpa Jones tell stories and play his music. Because this first event was such a success, local organizers decided to hold the tribute annually.

For more information, call 870/269-3851.

World Championship Quartz Crystal Dig

The vibe is good in Mount Ida. And it should be, it's crystal country. In fact, chances are good that the crystals from your last séance came from Montgomery County, Arkansas. There are so many "that after a good rain you can look down and see those little buggers everywhere," says Gayle Williamson of the Mount Ida Chamber of Commerce. Now, every October, the outside world gets the chance to get a little groovy, not to mention very muddy, by attending the World Championship Quartz Crystal Dig. Area crystal mines open their doors to the public for digging, and over $1,500 in prize money is given away to the best of the bunch. But hold on to your crystals, because you'll feel better with at least something to compensate for the $60 registration fee.

For more information, call 870/867-3785.

World Championship Duck Calling Contest

This annual event has been held every November since 1936, making it the oldest and most prestigious event of its kind in the nation. That first year only attracted seventeen contestants, and the winner, Thomas E. Walsh of Greenville, Mississippi, won without using a duck call. In other words, that old boy had the power to pull a duck out of his throat. Today, the contest is part of the weekend-long Wings Over the Prairie Festival, which attracts some 60,000 sportsmen from around the country. The contest is made up of more than sixty men and women who earned a spot in the world championship by winning one of the many regional duck-calling events held around the country every year; you don't have to use a prefab duck call, but 99 percent of the entrants do. Here they compete for a package worth more than $15,000. While callers must spend $50 to enter, the entire weekend is free for festivalgoers.

For more information, call 870/673-1602 or visit www.suttgartarkansas.com.

CALIFORNIA
COLORADO
CONNECTICUT

CALIFORNIA

Calaveras County Fair and Jumping Frog Jubilee

The Celebrated Jumping Frog of Calaveras County" (1865), the short story that first made Mark Twain famous, has also helped put the Calaveras County Fair and Jumping Frog Jubilee on the map. Although the fair debuted in 1893, the frog celebration wasn't an institution until 1928. Now it's the king daddy of all frog-jumping contests in America. Throughout the year, frogs and their ever-finicky human trainers compete at sanctioned events around the country in order to win a shot at this long-distance competition. Once they've earned their invitation, for three days every May, thousands of pairs of frog legs fly in Angels Camp; only fifty qualify for the International Frog Jump held on Sunday, where they have a chance at winning $5,000 if they beat the current world record of 21 feet and 5.75 inches, set in 1986 by Rosie the Ribiter, who was jockeyed by Lee Guidici of Santa Clara, California. First place in the jump takes home $750. Day tickets to the fair range from $8 to $10; a weekend pass can be purchased for $25. For kids under twelve and seniors over sixty-two, it's free.

For more information, call 209/736-2561 or visit www.frogtown.org.

ENOUGH SAID

Don't miss Brawley's annual Mariachi Festival held every November. **For details call 760/344-3160.**

Carpinteria

Avocado Festival

Did you know that when the Aztec ruler Montezuma presented a king's ransom to the Spanish explorer Cortés in 1519, he included avocados along with the gold, silver and priceless gems? The inhabitants of Carpinteria celebrate this history every year with a loony event completely centered around the "alligator pear." In fact, if you mention any other fruit or vegetable at this annual October event, you will be gutted, smashed and included in the World's Largest Bowl of Guacamole. Over 2,000 avocados are used to create this phenomenon, which feeds a crowd of approximately 12,000 hungry folks.

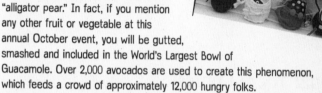

Founded in 1987 because Santa Barbara County is the third largest avocado producer in the country (Carpinteria being a major contributor), the Avocado Festival charges no entrance fee. Besides lots of chips and dip, visitors can partake in some friendly "avo-tivities." Of course there's a competition for the best guacamole and a variety of other avocado recipes, such as ice cream and brownies (just don't eat the facial scrub). And did you know that putting an avocado in a paper bag will speed the ripening process? But the biggest crowd pleaser is the Best Dressed Avocado, an idea undoubtedly stolen from the creators of Mr. Potato Head. Do I smell a lawsuit in the making? There's also a photography contest and pop-art show, where anything avocado goes. Holy guacamole!

For more information, call 805/684-0038 or visit www.avofest.com.

CAST YOUR VOTE FOR THE BEST-DRESSED AVOCADO

International Imitation Hemingway Competition

Known as the Bad Hemingway in erudite circles, this annual writing contest hopes to produce the best piece of Ernest Hemingway mockery the world has to offer. The only rules are that the writing sample must be no longer than one page, it must mention Harry's Bar & American Grill (Hemingway's favorite Italian watering hole), and it must sound and read like Hemingway while being side-achingly funny. The annual deadline for entries is in February, and the winners are announced in March at ... where else but Harry's Bar & Grill in Century City, California. Tickets for this dinner and awards ceremony are a whopping $125. A recent winner, Maxine Nunes, penned a Hemingway-meets-Lewinsky saucefest titled "Across the Potomac and Into Her Pants." Her prize? An all-expenses-paid trip for two to Harry's Bar in Florence, Italy. Bon appétit.

For more information, call 213/365-8500.

Chico

National Yo-Yo Contest

Shoot the Moon, Split the Atom, Time Warp, Singapore Sling and Velvet Rolls. These are the names of just several of the thousands of incredible yo-yo tricks you can see at the National Yo-Yo Contest held every October in Chico, otherwise known as the "Cooperstown of Yo-Yos." Since 1988 Bob Malowney, Director of the National Yo-Yo Museum, has hosted the event, which has grown to 200 entrants, both young and old, from around the country. "What used to be a toy is now a sport," Malowney says.

On three stages, contestants vying for a national championship slot compete in one of three categories: IA, which consists of only one-handed tricks; IIA, which consists of only two-handed tricks; and X, which consists of only extreme or experimental tricks. For those not interested in serious competition, there's the Recreational Class. While Malowney admits that the top players are usually between the ages of twelve and sixteen, he says some amazing seventy-plus men and women show up annually. "But they're not in it to win," he says. "There's just no way to compete against a fifteen-year-old. I mean, the kids have time to practice. The old guys have mortgages."

There is no fee to either compete or watch this annual event. Also free to the public are a vendors' and collectors' fair plus yo-yo demonstrations. "But the big draw for the kids," Malowney says, "is that every year one manufacturer introduces their new yo-yo at the contest."

For more information call 530/893-0545, extension 24.

Hacienda Heights

American Fancy Rat and Mouse Annual Show

I t's not uncommon for lovers of rats and mice to want to be taken seriously. Fine, they might love the little creatures, but they have big ideas. One of these is the American Fancy Rat and Mouse Association, which was founded in 1983. Now the AFRMA hosts many different mouse and rat shows around California every year, but the biggest is held in January—for the last several years in Hacienda Heights.

Just like any other animal show, judges evaluate rats and mice on standards set for each type of creature. The organization's goal? It's to promote and encourage the breeding and exhibition of fancy rats and mice as pets. Karen Robbins, a spokeswoman for the AFRMA, says, "Rats are very intelligent and can be trained like dogs. They are clean like cats— always washing themselves—and are very personable. They know their owners and want to be out with them." Mice, it seems, are not so smart and about as personable as guppies in a fishbowl.

CRAIG ROBBINS

MR. BIGGLESWORTH'S JERRY

For more information, call 818/992-5564 or visit www.afrma.org.

Absolut Chalk Street Painting Festival

I can't think of any better combination than vodka and chalk to really get the creative juices flowing. Every June since 1992, Absolut vodka and the Light-Bringer Project (a local nonprofit arts organization) have co-sponsored the Absolut Chalk Street Painting Festival, which is the largest festival of its kind in the world. It's a multicultural extravaganza of self-expression: four hundred of the world's best street artists descend upon Pasadena to paint—or shall I say chalk—two city blocks pink. Awards are presented in such categories as Wildest, Most Colorful, Best Rendition of a Master, Most Humorous, Most Inspiring and overall Favorite. Recent notable creations include a sixty-foot-wide red squid, a Chagall-style mural and a glow-in-the-dark scene of skeletons battling on horseback. Donated art, cash prizes and trips are commonly awarded. This festival attracts about 20,000 people, who not only ogle the art, but enjoy other cultural and musical events. Admission is $7.

For more information, call 626/440-7379.

Petaluma ▶

World Wristwrestling Championships

R oughnecks, meatheads and warlords have been arm wrestling for centuries. But serious competition didn't really begin until well after the reign of Ghengis Khan. It all began in 1953 when Petaluma hosted an event that has evolved into the Super Bowl of wristwrestling. Now every October, over 250 muscle mavens pay $20 to compete for $5,000 in prize money. An estimated 1,000 spectators pay $10 to see the afternoon eliminations and nighttime finals. "The reason we do it all in one day," says the stuttering Bill Soberanes, event coordinator, "is because the guys will have a sore arm the next day." Makes sense.

For more information, call 707/778-1430 or visit www.armwrestling.com.

World Championship Cribbage Tournament

This may not be one of the stranger events, but if you know someone who plays cribbage (read: an incredibly competitive tightwad who will do anything for a game), you know why I included it. During this annual May event approximately 350 contestants will pack twenty-two hours of cribbage into a weekend. Founded in 1972, this is America's oldest cribbage tournament, not to mention one of the world's largest, boasting a purse that averages over $25,000. The singles' entry fee is $60—$18 of which pays for brain food like coffee and donuts. Forty dollars will get your team a spot in the doubles tournament. And for all you cribbage losers (can there be anything worse!), $20 will get you a seat in the consolation tournament. Warning! Do not try this at home.

For more information, call 530/283-0800.

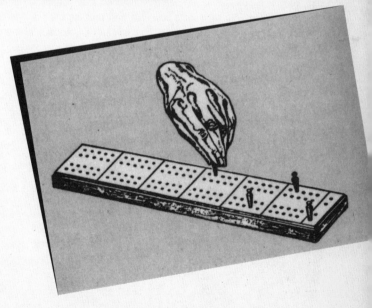

ArtCar Fest

Although San Francisco Bay Area artists Harrod Blank and Philo Northrup have been creating artcars for several decades, in 1997 they decided to team up and host the first ever ArtCar Fest. What is an artcar? "It's not a float," explains Blank, who has created two movies and a book on the subject. "We drive these cars everyday and they are extensions of our characters." Blank created his first artcar when he was seventeen, painting a rooster on the side of his 1965 white Volkswagen Bug. "I just felt so plain in a regular car," he says. "It just wasn't me." His creation stirred such a response from the public that he decided to take it to the next level. His second creation, the *Camera Van*, is a 1972 Dodge van with 1,705 cameras attached to the surface (including 10 working cameras) so that Blank can capture the way the public responds when he drives down the street.

About one hundred artcars from around the nation show up every October, including Larry Fuentes's *Cowasaki* (a life-size cow fastened to a motorcycle frame); Julian Stock's *Skull Car II* (a huge white cow skull built over the body of a compact car); and Northrup's own work in progress, *Truck in Flux* ("an abstract, ever-evolving creation"). The artcar created by the crowd on site is another highlight of the festival. Anyone who wants to can lend a helping hand.

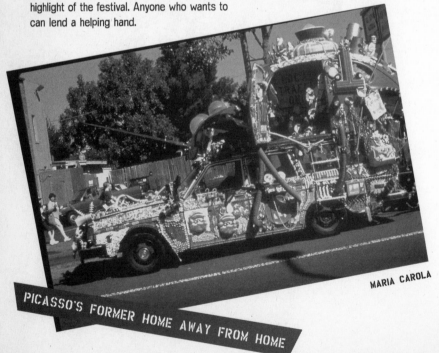

MARIA CAROLA

PICASSO'S FORMER HOME AWAY FROM HOME

In 1998 toys of every shape and size were attached to the body of a donated car, which fetched $300 in an auction. The lucky buyer proceeded to paint it black, then called it *Toys Were Us*.

In 1999, instead of having the public come to them, Blank and Northrup took the ArtCar Fest to the people via a traveling road show. Events were held in San Francisco, Berkeley, Oakland, and San Jose. "It's a missionary-type thing," Blank says. "We're taking our cars through all kinds of neighborhoods in a Fellini-esque parade. All of a sudden, this carnival just drives by and the audience is left thinking what the fuck was that!"

For more information, call 800/391-9673 or visit www.artcarfest.com.

San Francisco

San Francisco Zoo Valentine's Day Sex Tours

I f you're loveless this Valentine's Day, don't just sit at home playing with your monkey. Give your personal plaything a rest and venture to the San Francisco Zoo, where every V-Day penguin keeper Jane Tollini gives a live-action tour of how the real monkeys play. After noticing that penguins get a little horny every February, Tollini thought she'd have some fun. So in 1989 she cut out hearts to decorate the penguin pool, put some Johnny Mathis on the boom box and invited a select crew of friends and colleagues to enjoy the show. There's nothing like watching a little session or two of hide-the-sausage to make a crowd crazy. In fact, Tollini's bonanza of beastly butts and boobs has become so popular that it's a reservation-only affair; tickets go for $40 per four-hour tour, forty-five minutes of which feature the jungle-love train.

For more information, call 415/753-7080 or visit www.sfzoo.org.

U.S. National Handcar Races

Handcars are relics of railroad history, flatbeds on steel wheels that miners and track crews propelled by a hand pump. Truckee, home of the California State Railroad Museum, has celebrated this piece of its rich rail history every September since 1983 with the U.S. National Handcar Races. An average of thirty teams—five members each—pay $20 per person to enter. And there's no charge for spectators to witness these racers pump 1,000 pounds of handcar down a 1,000 foot-path to glory.

For more information, call 530/587-7474.

COLORADO

◀ Arapahoe Basin

The Cardboard Downhill Derby

Throw one more race into the random ski resort category: the Cardboard Downhill Derby. Whatever you want to make—a Bozo head, the Titanic, a biplane—you may use nothing more than cardboard, tape, glue and string. Held every February.

For details call 303/444-5600.

◀ Breckenridge

Ullr Fest

While this celebration of Ullr, the God of Snow (or the "Phat Man of Winter" as he's referred to locally) is predominantly a natives-only event, there's nothing keeping other ice heads from joining these free, wacky reindeer games. In fact, you're more than welcome to join the Ullympics—six days of sporting madness held every January. Each year about fifteen teams of four gather to compete in such events as the Four-Man Ski Race, in which each team navigates an intricate path on skis constructed out of two-by-six-inch pieces of wood. Or what about the Turkey Toss, where team members use a frozen turkey in a bowling event that's for the birds. While the Ullympics is just for fun, participants in the Ullr Parade have a chance at winning four free airline tickets. This is an anything-goes event, where the freakiest floats and the craziest costumes always catch the judges' eyes.

For more information, call 970/453-2913 or visit www.gobreck.com.

International Snow Sculpture Championships

O nce a part of Ullr Fest, this is now one of, if not the, most prestigious snow carving event in the world. It's held every January since 1991, and sixteen teams from countries including the United States, Argentina, Finland, Russia, Mexico, Canada and the Netherlands, to name just a few, are invited to compete. Chosen on the basis of their snow-carving credentials and drawings of proposed sculptures, each team is allowed sixty-five hours over a period of five days to scrape, chisel and shape (no electric tools permitted) a twenty-ton block of snow into a monstrous work of art. A panel of five judges then rates each sculpture on its quality, creativity, originality, use of medium and expression of theme. Gold, silver and bronze medals are awarded to the top three. Other awards include Artists' Choice, People's Choice and Kids' Choice. This is a free event.

For more information, call 970/453-2913 or visit www.gobreck.com.

CARL SCOFIELD

TWENTY TONS OF SNOW TURNED INTO ART

U.S. International Jousting Competition

ousting, some say, has been around since 1066. It's the age-old art of knocking your chain-mail-clad foe off his horse and onto his ass. Around the year 1200, a code of ethics developed between fighting men for the first time. This positive code of ethics became known as chivalry, a word that would be associated with knights ever after. Although jousting as a method of warfare soon became obsolete, jousting as a sport survived and spawned tournaments. In fact, the art of jousting is still revered around the world, especially at the U.S. International Jousting Competition held every September at the Longs Peak Scottish/Irish Highland Festival in Estes Park, Colorado. Some 50,000 people show up to witness not only jousting, but ring spearing, spear throwing and shield hitting. However, with a $1,400 purse to win, the jousting tournament is always the most exciting. Tickets are $15 for an adult and $5 for a child; an adult weekend pass goes for $42.

For more information, call 800/903-7837 or visit www.scotfest.com.

World Championship Pack-Burro Race

lthough pack-burro racing has existed in Colorado since the forties, it remains a homegrown sport that has happily avoided exploitation. Although some believe the origin of the sport dates back to Rocky Mountain miners who would race down from the hills to stake claims at the local courthouse, the truth is that it's just a revenue scheme thunk up by town do-gooders. It also is an impressive tribute to the spirit of the west—man and beast coming together to conquer the rugged terrain.

Pack-burro-racing rules state that each animal must carry a miner's pack containing a pick, a shovel and a gold pan. The total weight must be at least thirty-five pounds, often achieved by packing saddlebags with rocks and sand. A rope no longer than fifteen feet must connect each racer to his or her burro. In addition, the runner must maintain control of the burro throughout race's duration.

Often called the "Poor Man's PGA Circuit," seven pack-burro races take place annually between April and August, primarily in Colorado, with one in New Mexico and one in Arizona. Each town runs its race differently: Distances range from ten to twenty-nine miles and purses awarded to winners range from $1,000 to $5,000. In other words, a hot racer can turn a pretty penny following the circuit.

The world championships in Fairplay, just a part of their Burro Days celebration every July, is billed as the planet's "highest, longest, roughest and toughest" pack-burro race. Racers run twenty-nine miles with their burros, climbing 3,000 feet in all. (The town of Fairplay, population 500, is already at a 10,000-foot elevation.) Fifty-two-year-old Curtis Imrie is a two-time world champion who has missed only one of the seven annual races in the last twenty-six years. "It's arguably the toughest sport in the world," he says. "Mostly because of the beast. And I'm not just talking about the donkey. I'm talking about the beast within." He trains year-round, adhering to a strict seafood diet, plus putting in forty to sixty mountain miles of training every week. The New York City Marathon? It's child's play to Imrie. He says, "We have world-class runners that always come out and think they can pick up a little extra cash while training. We just laugh at them." While marathoners generally believe you should take a day off for every mile you run, pack-burro racers can't afford the luxury. They often cover over 130 miles of harsh, mountainous terrain in a ninety-day period.

Imrie is not only a champion pack-burro racer, he's probably the sport's biggest supporter. (He's also a writer, filmmaker and politician.) On his ranch in Buena Vista, Colorado, he keeps fifty burros, some of which are a new hybrid breed he created solely for the sport. He likens his burros to dogs and cats. "They bond with you every bit as much," he says. "They are so much smarter than horses. I think of them like having a four-year-old child around." But aren't burros notoriously stubborn? That's a myth that Imrie is devoted to dispelling. "Cautious is a better word," he advises.

If you're interested in racing, Imrie rents his mules by the season or by the race, which means any would-be racer from New York to California can have a well-schooled burro awaiting his or her arrival. He suggests that you start out at the race in Leadville, Colorado, which is a twenty-one-mile runner-friendly race.

**For more information call 719/836-2090
or visit www.gossamer-moon/curtisimrie.**

International Pack-Burro Race

ust across Mosquito Pass from the town of Fairplay is Leadville. The two towns used to organize the world championships jointly, agreeing to have the race finish in each town on alternate years. But like the Hatfields and McCoys, the two towns just couldn't get along, so they decided to host separate races. Leadville's annual race, a part of their Boom Days celebration, occurs every first full weekend in August.

For more information, call 719/486-3900.

BURRO RACER BARB DOLAN SPORTING SOME GOOD ASS

Emma Crawford Coffin Festival

Like many festivals across the nation, the story behind this one is rooted in local lore. In the late 1800s, the young Emma Crawford moved to Manitou Springs for the fresh mountain air and crisp, clean water. The town was a haven for health-seekers during that time, and Emma came seeking a cure for her tuberculosis. She fell in love with the town and its surrounding mountains and soon her fiancé, Mr. Hildebrand, joined her there. However, Emma's fight with the disease was short-lived: she died before she could marry. Respecting her last wish, Hildebrand and twelve men carried Emma's coffin to the top of the 7,200-foot Red Mountain and buried her. Emma rested peacefully in her spot of choice until the early 1900s, when heavy summer rains washed her coffin down the mountain and into the canyon below.

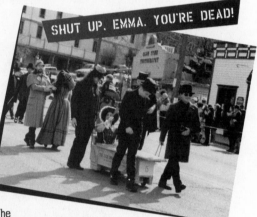

SHUT UP, EMMA, YOU'RE DEAD!

Every weekend prior to Halloween, the town of Manitou Springs hosts some morbid events in Emma's memory. The headliner of the memorial is the annual coffin race. Each team builds their own coffin and mounts them on tires that must be less than six inches in diameter. One "Emma" rides in the coffin while four others push their craft down a 250-yard stretch of Main Street. Besides speed, teams are also judged on the creative flair of their coffin design.

For more information, call 800/642-2567.

Society for Commercial Archeology Conference

The Society for Commercial Archaeology (SCA), founded in 1977, is the oldest national organization devoted to the artifacts, structures, signs and symbols of the twentieth-century commercial landscape. What does this mean? Member and Colorado organizer Mark Wolfe says, "Things that are developed to attract the traveling public." This includes the roads themselves and their counterparts like bridges and interchanges, plus gas stations, motels, theme parks, drive-in movie theaters ... you name it. About 150 people register to attend the conference annually, which involves three days of symposiums and guided tours. Most are part of the 800-member organization, but you don't have to be a member to attend. Members usually pay $95 for registration while nonmembers pay $120. Membership dues for the society run $25 per year.

Conferences are held every August. The 1999 conference, titled "Made in Ohio: Enameled Eateries, Durable Domiciles and Fast Food," included tours of the White Castle headquarters, the Longaberger Basket Company (the building is shaped like a basket) and the Kahiki Supper Club, which is one of many wildly unique Polynesian-themed restaurants that were popular after World War II. Tours cost extra and run about $50 per day, which includes all meals. The August 2000 conference will be held in Manitou Springs. Its title: "Automobile Culture in the Rocky Mountain West." Tours will include a trip up the cog railroad leading to the 14,110-foot summit of Pike's Peak; Santa's Workshop at the North Pole, a Christmas theme park that opened in the fifties; and the Will Rogers Shrine.

For more information, call 303/866-2776 or visit www.sca-roadside.org.

Great Fruitcake Toss

What do you do with that nasty fruitcake Grandma Glenda with the Elvis sideburns sends you every Christmas? You can take it to the Great Fruitcake Toss. Held every first week in January since 1995, all come not to pay homage to the fruitcake, but to hurl, dissect and destroy the damn things, not to mention to make fun of the people who gave them to you. You can compete in any number of events. There's tossing (by hand), launching (by catapult) and hurling (by any other method); a Fruitcake Derby (fruitcakes with wheels); a Fruitcake-Art Show (recent entries have been a stoplight and a Chia Pet, both carved from unwanted fruitcakes); the Farthest Traveled Fruitcake (fruitcakes have recently arrived from Hong Kong and New Zealand); and the obligatory Fruitcake Relay. A mere $5 will grant you entry to all events you wish to compete in. But remember, this is a BYOF party.

For more information, call 800/642-2567.

CONNECTICUT

This isn't your typical marathon. This is a reading marathon: every July, around 6,000 people show up to listen to a twenty-four-hour reading of Herman Melville's classic novel *Moby Dick*.

For details call 860/572-5315.

Stamford

American Crossword Puzzle Tournament

Although the first crosswords are said to have appeared in England in the nineteenth century, the award for the first published crossword puzzle goes to the American side of the pond. December 21, 1913, was the fateful day when *The New York World* newspaper bought its first crossword from journalist Arthur Wynne. In ten short years, the crossword spread across the nation. Today's foremost cruciverbalist—crossword constructor—is Will Shortz, who now hosts the American Crossword Puzzle Tournament, billed as the nation's oldest (since 1977) and largest crossword tourney.

Every March about 250 puzzlers show up to try their skills against other fanatics from around the world. Contestants, who are divided into eleven divisions based on age and skill, are scored based on accuracy and time. While most come to compete for the $1,000 grand prize, others come for the company and guest speakers, not to mention the free wine and cheese. While the weekend is open to the public, tickets to individual events range between $35 and $95. Entry to all the events plus the awards luncheon is $140.

For more information, call 732/274-9848 or visit www.crosswordtournament.com.

Boom Box Parade

For no other reason than just to be idiots, some 10,000 people turn out every July fourth for the Boom Box Parade, where folks with ghetto blasters in hand parade through the streets of this Connecticut town.

For details call 860/456-1111 or visit www.wili.com.

DELAWARE
DISTRICT OF COLUMBIA

DELAWARE

World Championship Punkin' Chunkin' Contest

What do small-town mechanics and machinists and welders do with their free time? They get drunk and think about how to throw shit real far. But these half-baked engineers add their own special flavor to the American bar scene. Between arguments over whose round it is, far-flung ideas, numbers and designs get scribbled on Pabst-soaked napkins. In fact, this might as well be a bar stool rule at watering holes around Lewes, Delaware, where, odds are, you'll find people trying to create machines to hurl pumpkins. That's because since 1986, Lewes has been the sight of the World Championship Punkin' Chunkin' Contest, held annually the first Saturday in November. The goal: Chunk that sucker the farthest without using explosives. Everything else is fair game. But what about outsiders? Should anyone with a punkin'-chunkin' contraption be able to waltz into Lewes and not only take the crown but beat the world record to achieve Guinness recognition?

Morton, Illinois, is the home of Matt Parker and his team of nine-to-fivers who created the Aludium Q36 Pumpkin Modulator, which looks more like a freaking tank than a device for winging melons. We're talking air-compression theory here, not some spring on a medieval manure catapult, but a weapon with the go-go to give a pumpkin a 4,026-foot boost and easily set the world record. That's almost a goddamn mile! No wonder Lewians are a little broken up. "At first I don't think they were very happy," Parker says. "There was a little animosity between the teams, but they took it pretty well. Now we call each other and send Christmas cards."

Pumpkin chunking may not be a respected American sport right now, but Parker and crew are doing all they can to spread the good word. They even recently demonstrated the Q36 on the *Late Show with David Letterman*, where they chunked pumpkins at New Jersey from the Manhattan side of the Hudson River. Can you say "squashed"? Admission to watch the contest in Lewes, which attracts a crowd of about 20,000, is $5. To enter your own pumpkin-chunking machine, event fees range from $5 to $50.

For more information, call 302/856-1444 or visit www.punkinchunkin.com.

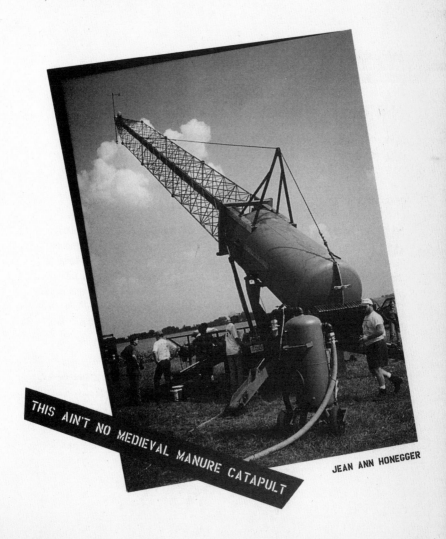

THIS AIN'T NO MEDIEVAL MANURE CATAPULT

JEAN ANN HONEGGER

DISTRICT OF COLUMBIA

National Geography Bee

Don't miss the finals of the National Geography Bee every May.
For details call 202/857-7001.

Canine Frisbee Disc World Finals

Most dog owners are pretty damn biased. "My mutt is an athletic genius," a friend recently told me. He thinks his furry friend is the best thing since flush toilets because she can catch a frisbee in mid air. I told him to put Abby to the test. From Lost Angeles, California, to Philadelphia, Pennsylvania, there are plenty of regional dog frisbee-disc competitions nationwide. The big kahuna is the Canine Frisbee Disc World Finals, held in D.C. every September since 1974, in which sixteen teams of finalists from the regional events compete for the crown. Open to all purebred and mixed-breed dogs, this is a free event, both for competitors and spectators. The grand-prize winner takes home a year's supply of canned and dry dog food and treats, plus a $1,000 U.S. Savings Bond. Crowd size is about 10,000.

For more information, call 800/423-3268 or visit www.ashleywhippet.com.

National Spelling Bee

Don't miss the finals of the National Spelling Bee every June. **For details call 513/977-3040.**

Potomac River Sacred Harp-Singing Convention

Every April a handful of God-fearing folks descend upon D.C. to churn out some church hymns. But these aren't any church hymns, these are the hymns from *The Sacred Harp* (1844), the most enduring of the shape-note tune books popular in nineteenth-century rural America. If fugue-ing tunes and anthems in unaccompanied four-part harmony in historic churches sounds like your idea of a horns-up rocking good time, then this is the place for you. (Read: You need to get out more.) Although the convention is dubbed free, "free-will offerings" are accepted.

For more information, call 301/897-5274 or visit www.his.com/~sabol/PRC99.html.

FLORIDA

Bonifay

All-Night Gospel Singing

Go get God in your britches at the Biggest All-Night Gospel Singing in the World. Always on the Saturday before the Fourth of July, this event attracts 10,000 Bible-belting songsters.

For details call 904/547-3613.

Fellsmere

NASRA Swampin' Series

Although the North American Swamp Racing Association is still in its infancy, swamp-racing has been around for about fifty years now. The fact that there are only about 115 swamp racers in America doesn't say much for the potential of the sport, but NASRA operations manager Mathew Graney is banking on his new organization to help legitimize the sport. He better hope it does, because the NASRA and the town of Fellsmere recently spent over 6 million bucks on Mesa Mark, a new fifty-acre motor-sports arena.

COURTESY OF NASRA

IT'S A CAR. IT'S A BOAT. NO. IT'S A BORED FLORIDA REDNECK.

The sport of swamp-buggy racing is a combination between a car and a boat race in fifteen inches of muddy water. The crafts, which fall into six different categories, are made by the racers and completely from scratch. As Graney says, "It's not like there's a swamp-buggy store where they can buy the skin. They build them from the ground up." In the Pro Mod class, for instance, crafts that have 1,000-horsepower engines and reach ninety miles per hour can cost up to $30,000 each. If you're thinking that speeds like that can make for some excellent end-over-end wipeouts, you're right.

Drivers each pay $50 to enter the races, which are held every January, July and September. The entire annual purse for the NASRA Swampin' Series is over $120,000, with an average of $4,000 going to each winner. For $14 a day ($25 for a weekend pass), you can witness the birth of a new extreme sport. You can also expect some good foot-stomping country and western entertainment from names like John Anderson and Neal McCoy.

For more information, call 877/466-2772 or visit www.nasra.com.

◄ Fellsmere

Fellsmere Frogleg Festival

t's hard to imagine frogs being the backbone of any local economy, but since 1990 they've kept the 2,500-person town of Fellsmere, Florida, from, well, croaking. All year round, green-gobbling hunters buzz up and down the St. John's River in their high-powered wind-boats trapping one hell of a load of hoppers. These are frozen until the third weekend of January when some 80,000 Kermit-loving old coots descend upon Fellsmere to swallow over 6,000 pounds of these crispy critters. "And we leave the toes on," says Beth Perez, chairwoman for the event. "We need those to pick our teeth." So, leave your fine dining duds, not to mention your blood-pressure gauges, at home. We're talking go grease mountain: a heap of fried frog legs, a mound of thick country grits, several golden brown hush puppies and a scoop of mayonnaise-heavy coleslaw. That's right, frog's legs are better than no legs at all!

For more information, call 561/664-0896.

Carnie Trade Show

-town, as this historic circus community is often referred to, was the home of the infamous Lobster Boy, who was gunned down by a hit man hired by his family. News about the murder and trial can be found in Fred Rosen's book *Lobster Boy*. It is still home to many freaks, including dwarfs, fat men, bearded ladies and human pin cushions. Many other circus and carnival folk live here as well, which makes it the perfect home for the Super Trade Show and Extravaganza which is the trade show for circus and carnival communities, held every February. While the show is expensive ($50) for the public to enter, a visit to Gibsonton during this annual event just might be your ticket to the strangest show on earth.

For more information, call 813/677-3590.

Fun-in-the-Sun Postcard Sale

very January, the National Postcard Society hosts the Fun-in-the-Sun Postcard Sale. It's the largest event of its kind in America, at which dealers sell antique and modern postcards to the public.

For details call 703/368-2757.

Interstate Mullet Toss

here's an art to throwing a mullet—a useless, bottom-feeding, saltwater fish. Since 1984, Pensacola locals and tourists alike have worked tirelessly to perfect this art. A year's worth of training, twelve-ounce curl after twelve-ounce curl, boils down to a single weekend of heated competition. Yes, I'm talking about the Interstate Mullet Toss held every April, where over a 1,000 people get sucked into the mullet mania and shell out $18 to toss a 1 1/2 pound fish. The entry money also gets you a T-shirt and a souvenir picture of you to send home: "Dear Ma, thanks for the college education!"

Barbara Burns is a bartender at the FloraBama Package & Lounge, one of the last great American roadhouses, which sits as much on Florida's soil as on Alabama's.

The tavern hosts this annual fish fest. "We throw 300 pounds of mullet from the Florida side into the Alabama side," Burns says. "Most people take the fish and roll it up like a baseball, tight as they can, crunch its little bones and everything else." Right away you'll recognize a mullet launched by an artist; it will slowly come unfurled and cut through the air, head first, and land about 150 feet away. Flings by regular folk often leave the mullet mangled, in many different parts. "We recycle," Burns boasts. "After you throw you have to retrieve your fish. And if it's not too screwed up, you wash it off and throw it back in the bucket." For the early-retired mullet, the FloraBama often invites some pelicans from the Alabama Wildlife Association to help clean up the mess.

How many people show up every year? "Let's just say we've got many many thousands," Burns says. "I never give that amount because the IRS would love to hear that." If you're interested in becoming one of the herd, there are lots of other events to look forward to. There's the Ms. Mullet Bikini Contest, a wet T-shirt contest, a hiney (butt) contest, volleyball, skeet shooting, a keg toss, three bandstands and seventeen bar stations. Burns commands, "Nobody goes without a cold beer or drink in their hand."

For more information, call 850/492-3048 (Florida) or 334/980-5118 (Alabama) or visit www.florabama.com.

Tampa

National Puppetry Festival

This is the head honcho of the various puppetry events around the nation, hosted by the Puppeteers of America, the oldest puppetry organization in the country, which was founded in 1937. Please make note: The festival occurs during the summer of every odd year, which means the next to-do isn't until July 2001. But have no fear string-twitchers, there are many regional festivals to choose from, which are listed on-line. Registration for the national event is $350 for nonmembers and $305 for members. Daily passes will be sold for about $75.

For further information, call 813/931-2106 or visit www.puppeteers.org

GEORGIA

Covington

The Dukes of Hazzard Fan Club Convention

Just good old boys, yep, that's Michael Streit and Aneesh Sehgal, president and founder of *The Dukes of Hazzard* Fan Club, which since 1998 has hosted a convention every July in various locations around the United States, but most recently in Covington. (*The Dukes of Hazzard*, starring the infamous Wopat-Schneider flaming-arrow-shooting duo and the lovely Miss Daisy, is a television series that aired from January 26, 1979, to February 8, 1985.) Streit is a certified Dukes' nut. "I've followed the show since its premiere," he says. "I've owned 1969 Dodge Chargers even before the series began. I've loved Chargers ever since I was a young kid, watching them drag race on the streets of my hometown of Aurora. It was a dream come true for me to see them selected as the bright orange 'General Lee' in a weekly TV series." God bless him!

Fans and freak-watchers alike will love this convention, where special guest appearances have included the likes of Ace Parker (the original moonshiner), Enos the deputy, and even Coo-Coo-Cooter, the friendly greaseball mechanic. On display are personal Dukes collections, rare memorabilia and titillating merchandise. This convention, which costs $30 for the public, is a little unorganized, so make sure you write or e-mail to confirm dates and locations.

The guys wouldn't release their phone numbers, so for further information, you'll have to write 1011 North Lake Street, Aurora, IL 60506 or e-mail DukesClub@aol.com.

World Gold Panning Competition

I n 1849 twenty years before the California Gold Rush, fortune seekers descended upon Dahlonega, beginning what locals call "America's first real gold rush." This small Appalachian mountain town is proud of its past. There are several 250-foot deep working gold mines open to tourists that brochures say produce "some of the purest gold in the world." For those interested in the history, there is also the Dahlonega Gold Museum to explore. But Dahlonega's claim to fame, at least as far as this book is concerned, is the World Gold Panning Competition, which has occurred every third Sunday in April since 1988.

Whether you're a local round-belly with a handlebar mustache or a ten-year-old city slicker from San Francisco, you can compete for the title of "World Champion Gold Panner." All you have to do is sift sand away from nuggets of gold faster than the Hatfields or McCoys.

For more information, call 706/864-7247.

Mountain Moonshine Festival

H idden from the kinfolk, deep within the Blue Ridge Mountains, backwoods brewers have been pumping out high-octane white lightning for over a century. But every October since 1968, in Dawsonville, Georgia, still-tenders, bar-backs, and liquor-heads of every ilk come down from the hills to celebrate (in public) the blinding brew best known as moonshine. Besides your token Elvis impersonator, cloggers, clowns and gospel singers, on site is a real still for the kids to climb on: "Look, Ma, no hands!" But the biggest draw has got to be the old-timers with a sour-mash-making history. And what about the drivers who used to outrun the cops with their trunks full of Georgia's finest funky juice? They are on hand, too.

For more information, call 706/265-6278.

The Summer Redneck Games

he crazy crew at the East Dublin, Georgia, rock 'n' roll/country music station Y-96 decided they needed to do something special in 1996. It wasn't just because they came in at 96 on the FM dial; no, it was also the year of the Summer Olympic Games in Atlanta. The brain trust came up with a plan: "The media kept saying that the Olympics were going to be run by a bunch of rednecks who didn't know what they were doing," says Mac Davis, one of Y-96's afternoon deejays. "So we figured if that's what the world expects, we'll give it to them."

The boys got together and came up with a schedule of events that would become the Summer Redneck Games, to be held every July. These events include the cigarette flip, the mud-pit belly flop, bobbing for pigs' feet, the big hair contest, the hubcap hurl, the seed-spitting contest, bug-zapper spitball, dumpster diving, and everyone's favorite, the armpit serenade. "That's when you cup your hand under your armpit and make farting noises," Davis says. "But people down here have taken it a step further and can play tunes." In 1998 one contestant pumped out the entire theme song to the television series *Green Acres*. Only 500 were expected to show up that year, but when 5,000 curious folk overtook this 2,000-person town, the organizers knew they had a hit. In its short existence, the Summer Redneck Games have been featured in the national media on *Fox Files*, *Good Morning America*, *The Maury Povich Show*, and MTV's *The Real World*.

A fixture at this annual event is a fellow by the name of L-Bow, a local asphalt technician who doesn't have any teeth. In his soiled bib overalls, smelly T-shirt, and ragged old shoes, L-Bow is the perfect mascot for the Summer Redneck Games, which means he's the official torchbearer. Of this honor, he sheepishly admits, "I got the big kiss and swole all up with pride." With a propane torch adorned with the aluminum from a six-pack of Budweiser, L-Bow parades the athletes into the arena (a field) and lights the Ceremonial Barbecue Grill. "Let the gas begin!" he hollers. Why do they call him L-Bow? "You see, every redneck has a nickname. And I make this ol' ugly face, putting my bottom lip up over my nose. One day when I was doing it, this ol' boy said, 'You just plain ugly from your elbow down to your ass. You don't look like the same person.' Well I said, 'You sure ain't going to call me ass, so I'll just take elbow.' And from that day on it stuck."

The event has raised controversy over the years. Some locals have come forward to say they think the term "redneck" is derogatory. Even some of the wine-and-cheese crowd have expressed their belief that the event is degrading. "You know what," L-Bow says, "everybody has a little bit of redneck in them. A redneck is anyone who works hard for every penny they get. It's the one time a year hard-working country folk in these parts can be proud of who they are and have a little fun." But don't think L-Bow is getting sentimental. "I got my own little creed about rednecks," he says. "We work hard, we play hard and we die broke." Gentlemen... put on your beer goggles and start your riding lawn mowers. Admission is $5 per carload, so pack 'em in.

For more information call 800/688-0096

or visit www.wqzy.com.

PATRICIA KIDD

BOBBING FOR PIGS FEET.

HAWAII

HAWAII

Hilo

World's Largest Hula Competition

Nothing will get you into the Hawaiian mood better than witnessing twenty-five of the best hula dancers on the island of Hilo shake their groovy things. Every April these dancers, either in individual or group categories, have seven minutes to show their stuff to a crowd of approximately 5,000 people. But this ain't no hooting and hollering event. Silence is sacred, so leave the bullhorn and cooler of beer at home. Tickets range from $5 for general admission to $23 for reserved seating.

For more information, call 808/935-9168.

Oahu

World's Greatest Lifeguard Contest

Lifeguarding for a living is nothing like *Baywatch* and, for these professional aqua enthusiasts, beaches aren't about buff bods, sun-blonde babes and tasty tans. However, for two days every June, lifeguards from around the world shuck their straight faces and strut their surf skills like Hollywood heroes. At the Hawaiian International Ocean Challenge they compete for the dubious title Best Lifeguard in the World. Teams from eleven countries including Great Britain, Japan, Canada and various teams from the United States vie for the crown in events like the 3.4 mile Paddleboard Race, the Outrigger-Canoe Race and the Surf-Rescue Swim, in which participants are timed towing a "drowner" a hundred yards to shore.

Hayden Kenny, the team leader for Australia, says the 4.3 mile Surfski (or ocean kayak) Race around Rabbit Island proves to be the toughest test for his team. His happy-drunk Aussie accent full blown, Kenny says, "It's that awkward kind, a bit short for endurance and too long to be called a sprint." Champs of the challenge for the past eight years, Kenny and the rest of his crew must be doing something right. But their secret is not much of a secret at all. "It all boils down to hard work," he says. "We train to be all-round lifeguards. Lots of swimming and paddling rescue boards and ocean kayaking. It's not good enough just to be a killer swimmer. You have to cross train." When asked about his competitors, a tinge of worry crops up in Kenny's voice. "New Zealand is looking really good, and I've seen a marked improvement in Hawaii and California." Although the total purse is $20,500, the winning team collects only $6,000. No one ever said being a lifeguard was a Fortune 500 gig.

For more information, call 808/521-4322 or visit www.teamunlimited.com.

COURTESY TEAM UNLIMITED

SURF RESCUE STUD

IDAHO
ILLINOIS
INDIANA
IOWA

IDAHO

Somewhere

Rainbow Gathering

The first Rainbow Gathering was held in 1972—the result of the peace movement and the back-to-the-land movement getting together to throw a celebration. Part of that first invitation reads as follows:

> "We, who are brothers and sisters, children of God, families of life on earth, friends of nature and of all people, children of humankind calling ourselves Rainbow Family Tribe, humbly invite: all races, peoples, tribes, communes, men, women, children, individuals—out of love; all nations and national leaders—out of respect; all religions and religious leaders— out of faith; all politicians—out of charity to join with us in gathering together for the purpose of expressing our sincere desire that there shall be peace on earth, harmony among all people."

What began as a one-time event has grown into an annual gathering of 20,000 tree-huggers that takes place every first week of July in a different national forest annually. But the entire event can last over two months, because hundreds of people show up early to help set up and stay late to break down. The Rainbow Movement has no doubt swept the nation: Handfuls upon handfuls of smaller gatherings occur across the nation year-round. (Since Jerry Garcia died, any time you see a throng of Volkswagen microbuses tooling down the highway, chances are there's a Rainbow Gathering near.) There are no membership qualifications, no fees or dues, no leaders, and virtually no rules other than one of peaceful respect.

Because the gathering takes place in the wilderness, people are asked to bring their own tent, sleeping bag, eating utensils and whatever else he or she thinks might add to the collective good of the gathering. Most often this is just a willing pair of hands to volunteer at one of the kitchens or a guitar to add song to someone's step. While all of the food is free, family members are encouraged to donate to the Magic Hat, which is passed around after every meal. Otherwise people might drum, dance, go on nature walks, search for wild herbs and mushrooms, barter, hang out, meditate, chant, talk politics or take part in body, mind and spirit healing exercises.

Locations for this annual celebration are not released until several months before the actual event. All I know is that, right now, the Rainbow Gathering for 2000 is scheduled for "somewhere in Idaho." But the family is very good about spreading the word. They have a massive presence on-line, which offers everything from maps to forest-service messages to weather reports to ride-sharing information.

For further information, write alwaysfree@welcomehome.org or visit www.welcomehome.org.

ILLINOIS

Byron

Turkey Testicle Festival

lthough a little tamer that the Testicle Festival in Bozeman, Montana, the annual Turkey Testicle Festival has been around longer. Since 1979 folks have been trotting to Byron every October to suck down some serious nuts—275 pounds worth of turkey testicles. What you may not know is that theirs' hang under the left wing rather than between the hind legs. How big are they? Human-size for the most part, but as with real men, some balls are bigger than others. Sponsored by the Union Street Station, a local bar, $3 gets you plenty to eat, plus lots of beer and bathroom humor.

For more information, call 815/234-9910.

"Weird Al" Yankovic Fan Convention

You have to expect that people weird enough to worship Weird Al will have a convention—it's known as ALCON. You remember Weird Al, right? He's the guy who's made a killing off his hilarious re-recordings of the day's hottest tunes. Those that made him famous in the early-eighties include "My Bologna," "I Love Rocky Road," and "Like a Surgeon." Some 250 fans of all shapes, sizes and genders showed up at the first convention in June of 1998. But ALCON is not an annual event: it's scheduled to be an every other year sort of thing. The next two gatherings are planned for May 2000 and May 2002. You can expect all kinds of Weird Al events, such as those honoring people like radio host Doctor Demento, who gave Weird Al his first break; an auction of unique Weird Al memorabilia; a Weird Al "look-Al-like" contest; a lip-synching contest (to Al's tunes, of course); plus a screening of Al's music videos and the movies he's starred and appeared in, such as *UHF* and *Desperation Boulevard*.

The biggest question is: Does the King of Weirdness show up? ALCON producer Amanda Cohen says, "In 1998 he surprised us. He showed up halfway through the day and made a big entrance while we were all watching a video interview with him on the big screen." While the vendor room is open for free to the public, to enter the main ballroom (the location for many of the events) and the video room, you must purchase a ticket. Tickets are $27 for Friday evening, $30 for Saturday, or $50 for both days.

For more information, call 312/552-4355 or visit www.come.to/alcon2000.

ALCON 2000

Old-Time Piano Playing Championship

No matter the population, towns and cities across America grab on to whatever sliver of public relations material they can use to help define their existence. We all do it. We all want to be somebody. And we are all judged by our achievements and failures, whether we like it or not. Decatur, Illinois, is no different. It has a population of 112,000 and defines itself in several different ways. First, Decatur is known as the Soybean Capital of the World, due to local food supplier Archer Daniels Midland. Second, Abe Lincoln had a home and law practice in Decatur before declaring his run for the presidency. Third, Decatur is the original home for the Chicago Bears football team. Finally, Decatur has been the home of the World Championship Old-Time Piano Playing Contest since 1975. Not bad for one town, huh? But what do these four things tell us about Decatur? Well, it's a community of politically minded farmers who think about the old days when they're not in front of the TV every Sunday afternoon.

Each May the town celebrates the world's finest old-time piano players, who get together to have a helluva good time while trying to pin down the $1,200 in prize money. The event begins with performances by thirty-two pianists, who each play two numbers in several rounds of single elimination. To make the competition fair, everyone plays on the same 1883 rosewood Weber upright named Moby Dink. While the contest is the main event, there are also old-time and ragtime music workshops, the World's Largest Sing-Along Party and Variety Show, plus a piano-dealer room and nightly parties.

For more information, call 217/428-2403 or visit www.members.tripod.com~oldtimepiano.

Milk Drinking Contest

G ot milk? Milk Days is the longest-running festival (since 1941) in the state of Illinois, and the 6,000-person town of Harvard is in the heart of the nation's dairy land. What better place to hold the Milk-Drinking Contest every June? Over 125,000 people show up to witness 100 people of all ages as they try to out mustache their brethren. This is a progressively difficult event: eight-to-eleven-year-olds must drink a half a pint of whole milk; twelve-to-thirteen-year-olds, a pint of two-percent milk; fourteen-to-seventeen-year-olds, a pint of whole milk. Those over eighteen years old must drink a quart of whole milk. The last age group proves to be the biggest crowd pleaser because of an annual rivalry between two of the fastest milk drinkers in the nation: Chad Odling and Pat Thoele. But no matter who wins, each year both men celebrate together with a dual milk upchuck after the show. For what? A mere $25 and some lame donations by local shops.

For more information, call 815/943-4614 or visit www.milkdays.com.

Mattoon

BagelFest

M attoon is the home of marvelous Murray Lender, whose local Lender's Bagels Factory employs most of the town. Thus you can see why in Mattoon there is no God but the Murray-man and his bread of heaven. Since 1986 Murray has hosted BagelFest very July. It's a weekend-long event dedicated to the almighty. Some 40,000 people show up for Murray's largest free bagel breakfast in the world, where they down approximately 70,000 bagels. For the Tenth Anniversary BagelFest, Murray set out to make the world's biggest bagel; at a whopping 563 pounds, it made *The Guinness Book of World Records*. But that didn't stop old Murray: Put a little fire in a man's pants and it's tough to put out. In 1998 Murray made "The World's Berry Biggest Bagel," which weighed in at an unbelievable 765 pounds. So, what's this man around Mattoon got up his sleeve next? Well, that's a secret. You'll have to roll to BagelFest to find out. (It also mustn't go unsaid that the Glenn Miller Orchestra and the Tommy Dorsey Orchestra have entertained at recent BagelFests.)

For more info call 217/235-5661.

STA-BIL National Lawn Mower Races

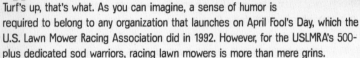

KEN JONES

What happens when a weekend chore becomes competitive sport? Turf's up, that's what. As you can imagine, a sense of humor is required to belong to any organization that launches on April Fool's Day, which the U.S. Lawn Mower Racing Association did in 1992. However, for the USLMRA's 500-plus dedicated sod warriors, racing lawn mowers is more than mere grins.

STA-BIL, a Gold Eagle Company fuel stabilizer, annually sponsors ten regional mow downs in cities from Atlanta, Georgia, to Swiftwater, Pennsylvania. But the main event is held in Mendotta, Illinois, every September. Racers compete in three road-track classes, which are Factory Stock, Prepared and Factory Experimental. In each class, the lawn-mower blades are removed for safety. Mowers in each category reach speeds up to 10, 35 and 60 miles per hour, respectively. The machines have names ranging from Sodzilla to Turfinator to Lawn Ranger to Garden Gangster.

Bobby Cleveland is probably the world's most famous lawn-mower racer, a three-time STA-BIL National Prepared-Class Champion, who has been racing for the past twenty years. An employee in the design and engineering department at Snapper, Cleveland boasts, "I built a lawn mower that would go seventy-five miles per hour all the way back in 1976." Wearing two hats, both as racer and spokesperson for the U.S. Lawn Mower Racing Association, Cleveland does quit a bit of traveling with team member Mark Boyce, both of the BC Racing Team. "We got a thirty-three-foot Pace Arrow motor home with twenty-foot trailer that carries four mowers and a golf cart," Cleveland, certified mow maniac, says. In a year he competes in anywhere from fifteen to twenty races, plus makes stops at many other fairs and parades around the country. "On one of my machines, I can ride a wheelie at twenty-five miles per hour," he adds. "That's always popular at parades."

Cleveland, like most mow enthusiasts, does all the work on his machines. Although he claims to have about $2,000 invested in each, he says most people get away with spending between $300 and $400 per machine. "But the best thing about the sport," he says, "is that anybody can take the blades off their machine, put on a helmet and race." While it hasn't happened yet, race organizers are planning on having mowers available for rent at each event. Racing fees range anywhere from $5 to $30, but you don't have to pay a dime to become one of 2,000-plus spectators who show up in Mendotta to witness America's fastest mowin' sport. The mow the merrier.

For mow information, call 847/729-7333 or visit www.letsmow.com.

Superman Celebration

It's a bird, it's a plane, no it's just a pitiful little town looking to make a buck off its name. Although Metropolis, Illinois, literally has nothing to do with Superman, they bank on the fluke of a shared name for some serious revenue. And why not, they are the only Metropolis listed in the United States Postal Code Directory. But the super-hero road hasn't been so easy. In the early seventies, before the Superman movies made the caped crusader big business, Metropolis was declared the Hometown of Superman by the Illinois House of Representatives. The local Superman Association got to work raising funds to erect the Amazing World of Superman, the only Superman museum in America. However, after a couple of years, the museum went bankrupt and all of the Superman paraphernalia they had acquired was auctioned to the public and scattered across America.

The year 1978 brought new hope. When the first Superman movie was released, the town was inundated with telephone calls: "Umm ... can you tell me Superman's address?" Eager to put its name back on the map, Metropolis founded the Superman Celebration, held every June, and a fifteen-foot bronze statue of Superman was erected in the center of town. So what will you see here? Expect to get a glimpse of about anything you can possibly imagine having to do with America's most well-known super hero. Also on hand every year are Superman comic-book artists, plus actors who on TV or in films have played Lois Lane, Jimmy Olsen or the Man of Steel himself.

For more information, call 800/949-5740 or visit www.metropolischamber.com.

STEVE SCHLAGER

THE HEARTLAND SUPERHERO

TRUTH – JUSTICE – THE AMERICAN WAY

Punkin' Chunkin' Contest

This ain't the real thing, but the gods of the throw found their humble beginnings in mini Morton, Illinois. That's right, Matt Parker, Chuck Heerde, and the rest of the Aludium Q36 Pumpkin Modulator team (see page 40) are homegrown heroes who landed in *The Guinness Book of World Records* for their 4,491-foot throw. Although bigwigs now, the Q36 crew hasn't forgotten their humble Morton roots. Every October you can catch them here warming up for the World Championships.

For more information, call 309/266-5337.

Quincy

World Freefall Convention

The World Freefall Convention (WFFC), a wild weekend of wine, women and song, is like no other party on the planet. That's because it celebrates the extreme sport of skydiving. And I'm not talking about the way your gramps used to jump from a plane in World War II. No, this is "The World's Largest Boogie," which means naked jumps, jumps in rafts, sky surfing and lots of radical dudes and dudettes screaming "Hell yeah, Bro!" from 23,000-foot altitudes.

This annual event has taken place every August since 1990 on a desolate Illinois airfield surrounded by miles and miles of wide-open spaces. Here's some statistics from the 1999 WFFC. It drew 5,410 registrants, which included both jumpers and nonjumpers from all fifty states in America and fifty-two countries. Over 65,000 jumps were made in ten days, including 503 tandem jumps. Eighty-four Accelerated Freefall School (AFS) students made the grade. Legendary skydiver Mike Burt made 180 jumps, 393 kegs of beer were given away, seventy-six units of blood were collected, and $30,855 was raised for various charities.

Registration to the WFFC is $49 for jumpers and $24 for nonjumpers. This basic fee gets you free camping, hot showers, seminars, nightly entertainment, and most importantly, all the beer you can put away. (The beer tents don't open until the last jump of the day has landed.) If you want to jump, you'll need a "B" license, which is the equivalent of AFS training and fifty jumps, and a USPA (United States

Parachuting Association) membership, which you can buy on site for $8. A single jump from a hot-air balloon costs $79, while one from a helicopter goes for $39. The best deal is the Ten-Pack Standard-Jump Ticket, which will cost you $170. First-time jumpers have two opportunities. You can either jump tandem ($159), with someone attached to your back, or you can take the multi-day AFS school, which will cost you almost $700.

No matter how you look at it, skydiving is dangerous as hell. Convention organizer and AFS instructor D. Jan Stewart says, "There is a tragedy almost every year. This past year a young jumper broke his femur in a corn field. He had passed away by the time someone found him several hours later. And breaking a leg is, unfortunately, a frequent occurrence." But it's not just the jumpers who are in danger. Another frequent occurrence is jumpers falling from the sky, skipping off the tops of mobile homes and ripping through lunch tents. Whether you are a jumper or a lawn-chair spectator, prepare to keep your eyes to the sky and your *cojones* in your throat. The WFFC is one of the ballsiest gatherings in this book.

For more information, call 217/222-5867 or visit www.freefall.com.

INDIANA

Big Whopper Liar's Contest

When I call Jeff Fleming about the Big Whopper Liar's Contest, he says, "You're in the wrong place, buddy. Who you trying to reach again?" After a little more back-and-forth, I realize he's doing what he does best—pulling the wool over my ears. Every third Saturday in September since 1988, men and women have gathered in New Harmony to celebrate the tall tale. The event was started by local trickster Aubry Robison, Jr., but after his death several years ago, Fleming took over the helm. About fifteen contestants take the stage in front of a crowd of maybe 400. They get four minutes to spin the most incredible yarn they can come up with. A team of judges award points for exaggeration, humor, stage presence and storytelling ability. This event, which will cost contestants and spectators alike $5 to enter, is now a part of Kunstfest, a weekend-long German period festival.

For more information, call 618/395-8491.

Circus City Festival

In the late 1800s, puny Peru, Indiana, was the winter holdover for seven of the world's major circuses. Rumor has it that local Peruvian Ben Wallace housed one of these circus's wild animals in his livery stable. When the circus master defaulted on the feed bill, Wallace acquired a blind lion, a trained baboon, a bevy of birds, a cage full of monkeys, plus an assortment of costumes. And what did the smart guy do? That's right, he started his own circus. Although wayward Wallace was a whopping circus success story, his name was all but erased from clown-town textbooks until the Circus City Festival revived his history in 1958, when it was founded. Now an annual event, the festival occurs every July.

But this isn't an ordinary circus, it's the oldest and largest youth (ages seven to twenty-one years) big-top performance in the country. Here, in a three-ring building near the center of town, some 250 young people prepare every summer of every year to pull off the Greatest Teenybopper Show on Earth. Events include the flying trapeze, high-wire, High and Low Casting, teeterboard and other favorites. Some of the kids traditionally go on to careers with Ringling Brothers. And the Shrine Circus. In 1998 a team of tumblers at the Circus City Festival performed an eight-person pyramid and landed it perfectly, a feat that landed them in *The Guinness Book of World Records*. The only question is why would any parent want to encourage the possibility of their kid working in a circus? Whatever the reason, it's a lot of good clean fun for the whole family. (To get a better glimpse of this oddball world, check out the documentary *Circus Town U.S.A.*) Tickets for performances range from $4 to $8 for children and $5 to $9 for adults.

For more information, call 765/472-3918.

Popcorn Festival

While popcorn itself isn't so odd, the world's most famous popcorn popper Orville Redenbacher is, or was—rest his hot-buttered soul. Who could forget that nerdy rail of a man with his big fat bow tie? Each Saturday following Labor Day, the town of Valparaiso, Redenbacher's hometown, celebrates his legacy at the Popcorn Festival. Every year some 70,000 people show up at this free event to put the almighty popped kernel on the pedestal. While there's lots of popcorn on hand to eat, you can also learn creative ideas for decorating with popcorn. Who would have thought? But the big event is the popcorn parade, where float designers are encouraged to use popcorn on their crafts. A float in the 1979 parade, the first year of the event, was a popcorn ball with a twelve-foot diameter, which made it into *The Guinness Book of World Records*.

For more information, call 219/464-8332 or visit www.popcornfest.org.

IOWA

National Hobo Convention

Yes, they're still out there. Uncounted tens of thousands of freight-hopping hobos still crisscross the country every year for free. Although rumors have been purporting the extinction of the American hobo for the last century—due to railroad mergers, new car designs and beefed-up rail-yard security—these vagabonds are alive, and for the most part well, at least at the National Hobo Convention in Britt, Iowa, which dates all the way back to 1900. Every August some 20,000 farmer-tanned folks descend upon this one-horse hamlet to gawk, giggle and learn from hundreds of hapless hobos. From retired graybeard relics of the steam-train era to full-time rail riders fresh from the tracks, they each have a story to tell.

The best place to begin your journey is the Britt Hobo Jungle, which is nestled against the Soo Railroad Line at the northern edge of town. The jungle is the center of all the action. It has a

MR. BOJANGLES AND WINDY CITY TOM

NELSON TAYLOR

pavilion, a stationary boxcar tagged by past travelers ("If our country is really against war, why don't we have a Secretary of Peace?"), plus lavatories and showers where the soiled travelers can sally before being cast into the spotlight, though many, like Iowegian Rick and Aussie, stand tall—grease, grime and all. This is also where hobos pitch their duct-taped tents, tie their tarps between two trees or just sack out for the night on a box under the stars. It seems like there is always at least one campfire with a pot of coffee wedged into the coals. And if you're patient, Mr. Bo Jangles, Liberty Justice, Windy City Tom or Danville Dan might pull up a stool, stoke the fire and pick some serious Woody Guthrie songs.

Throughout the weekend, there are scheduled hobo jams (seems like they all play at least one instrument), auctions of hobo paraphernalia (like a monkey's paw necklace or a signed collection of hobo poems) and storytelling. For an edgier experience, don't miss the hobo theater, where the younger generation act out R-rated scenes from their encounters on the rails. And don't forget about the Hob Nob, one of two watering holes in town that caters to the hobos. But be careful: as the beer consumption increases, so does the possibility of a bar-clearing brawl. Every year at least five or six hobos spend the entire convention in the Britt jail for intoxication-related infractions.

The highlight of the entire weekend is the annual crowning of the King and Queen of the Hobos at the Municipal Park at the center of town. This is a hilarious event. The crowd is warmed up with a free meal of 400 gallons of mulligan stew—a traditional hobo dish akin to chili made from whatever is available, from a can of beans to a freshly killed squirrel. Volunteers and Boy Scouts ladle out this soupy concoction from huge, human-size pots. But don't be shy. The chef definitely knows what he's doing. As you bask in the sun, watching a hobo or two doing a mountain jig, those running for king and queen will begin to ascend the pavilion stage. The candidates get several minutes to make a speech before the din of applause determines the winners. Then it's hugs and high-fives amid snapping flashbulbs.

Because hobos are one of the last authentically American breeds, the news media is often out in force to catch a glimpse of these yesteryear roustabouts. You might see a crew from CNN, a writer from *Spin*, a photographer from *Life* or a team of foreign filmmakers shooting a documentary. Once the king and queen have posed for their last photo in full ceremonial regalia, (red cloaks and crowns made from Folgers' cans), if you're brave, follow the crowd back to the Hob Nob. While you won't find the winners sucking down dollar drafts—they're too busy greeting the public—it's the last great opportunity to shoot the breeze with past official kings and queens like Frog and Minneapolis Jewel (1998) or New York Slim and Cinders (1999) or any number of hobos who are kings and queens, at least until the hangovers hit.

For more information, call 515/843-3867.

KANSAS

Coffeyville

Dalton Defender Days

Every October, on the weekend closest to the fifth—the day in 1892 that the infamous Dalton Gang tried to rob two banks at the same time in their own town (that's smart) and lost their lives—the town of Coffeyville put on Dalton Defender Days. But it is not a celebration of the Daltons, it's a celebration of the four citizens who took up arms against the Daltons and lost their lives. Come meet some of the relatives of those brave men—Lucius Baldwin, George Cubine, Marshall "C.T." Connelly and Charles Brown—or head to the Dalton Defenders Museum where you can see three saddles used by the outlaws, Bob Dalton's single-action Colt-45 revolver, a sack used to carry the money stolen from one of the banks, some of the gang's clothing and even the threshold from the old First National Bank. Don't forget to go outside where you can witness a re-enactment of the events of that fateful day, which left a total of eight dead and put Coffeyville on the map forever. The weekend is entirely free and attracts about 5,000 people annually.

For more information, call 316/251-1194 or visit www.coffeyville.com.

Pony Express Festival

his festival, sponsored by the Kansas State Historical Society, celebrates the history of the Pony Express, a service founded in 1860 that proved mail could be carried to and from the West faster than anyone had thought possible. Even though the company that started the Pony Express was charging upwards of $5 for each letter one-half ounce or less plus regular postage, their costs far exceeded their revenues. Then in October of 1861, the Pony Express was superseded by telegraph. The most westerly station, just outside Hanover, is the Hollenberg Station, which is the site of the annual Pony Express Festival held every August. This free event includes lots of Bible-thumping, music by such outfits as the Horseshoe Farmers Band, plus living history demonstrations and displays.

For more information, call 913/337-2635.

 LaCrosse

Kansas Barbed Wire Swap

ot a killer collection of barbed wire? An all-points bulletin: Get your butt to the Kansas Barbed Wire Swap held annually the last weekend in April.

For details call 785/222-9900.

 Liberal

International Pancake Day Race

his is a fifty-year-old competition between the women of Liberal, Kansas, and Olney, in the United Kingdom, where the competition is a 500-year-old tradition. Every March in each town, all those interested in entering compete to uphold the integrity of pancake racing. At the sound of the starting gun, the women, each holding a skillet, must first flip their pancakes. Then they sprint through the 415-yard course, then flip their pancake again after crossing the finish line. Once the winners are declared, the two towns call each other on the telephone to determine which country gets the syrup-sticky trophy. The reigning champion is Liberal's Sheila Turner. Her run of 58.5 seconds, which dates back to 1975, helped Liberal earn its nickname: Pancake Hub of the Universe.

For more information call 316/626-0170.

KENTUCKY

World Championship Bourbon Barrel Relays

An estimated ninety-five percent of the world's bourbon is made in Kentucky, which gives the term brown water new meaning. In other words, whiskey flows like water here, so it's not uncommon for half the state to be glassy eyed and stumbling any time of day or night. This is especially true every September during the Kentucky Bourbon Festival in Bardstown, home to thirty-two operating bourbon distilleries with records dating back to 1776, making Bardstown the undisputed Bourbon Capital of the World.

Since 1991 Bardstown has also been the site of the World Championship Bourbon-Barrel Relays. Bill Friel, the master distiller at Barton Brands, Limited and creator of the event says, "We took the liberty of calling it the World Championship because it's done nowhere else in the world." It's early morning and Friel sounds as if he had bourbon instead of milk in his Wheaties. Some fifty men and women from local distilleries—Jim Beam, Wild Turkey, Heaven Hill and Maker's Mark to name a few—compete by rolling 500-pound barrels through the rectangular forty-by-twenty-eight-foot course called a rick, which is the common term for the rack in which bourbon barrels are placed in the warehouse. "This part in the production process is still run by manpower," Friel says. "There's no way a machine can get the set right." You see, each barrel has a bung hole in its belly that must be in the upright position to avoid leaking. Because the barrel-relay venue only holds an audience of 250, make sure to arrive early.

Other events throughout the weekend include free tours of local distilleries, a night of bourbon tasting ($100 per person), a free lecture on the science of bourbon and a bourbon cooking class ($40). Bardstown is also the home of the Oscar Getz Museum of Whiskey History.

For more information, call 800/638-4877 or visit www.bardstowntourism.com.

450-Mile Outdoor Festival

his event is original because it doesn't take place exclusively in Covington, Kentucky. It starts there and ends 450 miles away in Gadsden, Alabama. The route is the U.S. Highway 127 Corridor and Lookout Mountain Parkway. And it isn't really a festival: It's more like the world's largest yard sale, held annually over a long weekend in mid-August. Some 100,000 people stop and browse through the seemingly endless array of junk. The tourism departments for Alabama, Kentucky and Tennessee all get together to pull this off. Why? They want the rest of the world to witness the historic, back-road towns of the south—and, of course, increase their revenue. It's all a ploy to rob rich folks blind.

For more information, call 800/327-3945 or visit www.kentuckytourism.com.

Hopkinsville

Edgar Cayce Convention

f you have something that ails you, join other Edgar Cayce cult fanatics every March in the town where he was born. Cayce (1877–1945) was known as the Sleeping Prophet because of his ability to put himself into an altered state of consciousness in which he could access a world of knowledge. People flocked to him to ask questions about their mental and physical health. It is claimed that Cayce always had the cure. Come listen to Cayce scholars, meet Cayce's relatives, and take a tour of local Cayce sites. The cost for this three-day event, which includes the seminar, meals and a theater ticket, is $135.

For more information, call 270/887-4270.

Lebanon

Country Ham Days

ome to the annual Country Ham Days held every September in order to help a crowd of 50,000 porkers put away 600 pounds of pig.

For details call 270/692-9594 or visit www.hamdays.com.

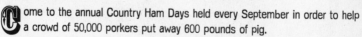

World Chicken Festival

Even from the grave, the Colonel is stirring up an original recipe of kooky clucker contests at the World Chicken Festival. Colonel Harland Sanders, bless his finger-licking soul, opened up his first Kentucky Fried Chicken joint here in Lauren County in the forties. Now hordes of his fast-food followers (250,000 these days) come to downtown London, Kentucky, every September to celebrate his legacy. This baby is entirely free to spectators. However, if you want to eat some chicken, it'll cost you; that's unless you're entered in one of the chicken-wing-eating contests.

All of the chicken for the event is cooked in the World's Largest Skillet, which is ten feet, six inches in diameter, eight inches deep, with an eight-foot handle. The entire weight of the beast is just over 700 pounds. One chicken fry uses 300 gallons of oil to produce 600 extra-crispy quarters. Other events include the Colonel Sanders look-alike contest (first prize is $300), plus rooster crowing, strutting and clucking competitions.

For more information, call 800/348-0095 or visit www.chickenfestival.com.

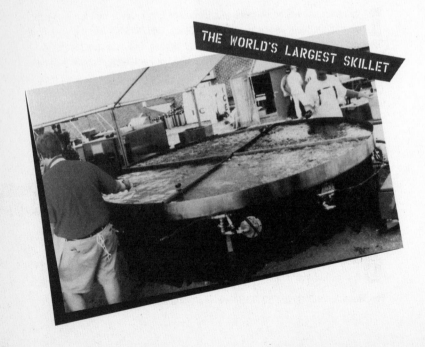

THE WORLD'S LARGEST SKILLET

National Quartet Convention

his is the oldest Southern gospel-quartet convention in the nation, held every September since 1957. It is also the largest, attracting crowds of up to 60,000, who pour into the Kentucky Fair & Expo Center's Freedom Hall to hear some eighty quartets belt out their religious songs. Also on hand are pulpit-pounding motivational speakers, plus musical and spiritual vendors (Bible salesmen). The $20 ticket price is worth all the laughs you'll get from all the bad hairpieces.

For more information, call 800/846-8499 or visit www.natqc.com.

Coaster Con

he American Coaster Enthusiasts (ACE) organization holds many different roller-coaster events around the country. Their biggest, Coaster Con, held annually in June, will take place at Six Flags Kentucky Kingdom in 2000. The location for 2001 was not scheduled at press time.

For details about this or other ACE events call 415/643-3843 or visit www.aceonline.org.

Running of the Rodents

There's no better way to take a break from the rat race than . . . racing rats.
Begun in 1972 by a science professor at Spalding University, the annual
Running of the Rodents (which takes place in April, just weeks before the Kentucky
Derby) is all part of campus Rat Week. But it isn't all fun and games. The care
and training of the rats teach students important information about behavior-
modification techniques. Whatever that means, right? Anyway, toss away all the
erudite mumbo jumbo and you've got yourself a humdinger of a hotwheelin'
hoopla. While outsiders are not welcome to race their own rodents (read: fear of
unnaturally enhanced sewer sleaze), regular folks like you and I can take part in
the Rodent Parade, the Rat Hat Contest, and the Fruit-Loop Eating Contest. Why
Fruit Loops? Rats go hog-wild over them, of course.

For more information, call 800/896-8941.

 Westpoint

World's Largest Machine Gun Shoot

Men love guns. In the south men and women love guns. In Kentucky men
and women and children and their dogs love big friggin' guns able to turn
an old refrigerator to scrap. For a long weekend twice a year (in April and October),
an estimated 10,000 folks come out of the woodwork for the World's Largest
Machine Gun Shoot in Westpoint, Kentucky. Most bring high-tech weapons like
AK-47s, M-16s and Maxim guns. Others bring some real heavy-duty shit. Kenny
Sumner, whose father started the shoot in the early seventies, says, "Whatever
they can bring in here they can shoot." Tanks? Yes, a tank or two always make an
annual appearance, and yes, they consistently blast an old beater off its wheels.

But you don't have to be a militia member to enter the grounds of the Knob Creek
Gun Range. Anybody with $7 can come in. Machine guns can be rented for $15
and, if flames are your game, try a flamethrower out on a Chevy Impala for about
$50. If you're hankering for a little competition, for $25 you can borrow a pistol or
a shotgun and maneuver through a police-training course, blowing away silhouettes
of bad guys. There is also the Sub Gun Jungle Walk ($10), where contestants run
rather than walk through a course searching for hidden targets to blast with a

sub—machine gun capable of letting loose 600 to 800 rounds per minute. But the highlight of the event is the Saturday Night Shoot, when the whole crew gathers to wield their weapons and light up the night. "It's sort of like the Fourth of July with machine guns," Sumner says. "It's a big barrage of tracer bullets and flames, a nice solid roar of weaponry."

While you won't find any cultural fluff like arts, crafts, entertainment or local cuisine, there are guns, guns and more guns. Exhibitors from all over the world spread out their motley munitions on 600-plus eight-foot tables for buying, selling and swapping. Who knows, maybe those of you who show up without a machine gun may decide to go postal and pick up your first ultimate Uzi.

For more information, call 502/922-4457 or visit www.machinegunshoot.com.

CEASE FIRE! IT WAS JUST A FRISBEE

MARIA CAROLA

LOUISIANA

LOUISIANA

Giant Omelette Celebration

Did you know that the omelette is an international symbol of friendship? Walk up to a Frenchman, who are notorious for disliking Americans, offer an omelette, any old kind will do, and be prepared to have a friend for life. It's that easy. The power of the omelette is immense. Since 1985 when Abbeville, Louisiana, held its first omelette celebration, the town has been a member of the worldwide fraternity of the omelette. They joined the sisterhood of cities such as Bessieres, France; Quebec, Canada; and Malmédy, Belgium, which send ministers of the omelette to Abbeville every November to help the locals cook the world's only Giant Cajun Omelette. This Omelette of Friendship, as it is called, is given away to all who attend. Ingredients? To start, try 5,000 eggs, fifty pounds of onions, seventy-five bell peppers, 6.5 gallons of milk, fifty-two pounds of butter, three boxes of salt and two boxes of black pepper.

The legend of the omelette dates back to the times of Napoleon. When he and his army were traveling through the south of France, they decided to rest for a night near the town of Bressieres. Napoleon dined on an omelette that evening. He thought it such a culinary coup, he ordered that all of the eggs in the village be rounded up for a giant omelette to feed his troops. About 5,000 people show up every year for this free event.

For more information, call 318/893-6517.

World Famous Breaux Bridge Crawfish Festival

No doubt, Louisiana is the crawfishiest state in America. And on the banks of the Bayou Teche, the small community of Breaux Bridge goes mud-bug mad every first weekend in May. In fact, Breaux Bridge became world renowned in 1959 when 5,000 crawfish-loving crazy Cajuns celebrated its centennial with such verve that the Louisiana State Legislature passed Concurrent Resolution Number 17, which named the town *La Capitole Mondiale de l'Ecrevissé*, or "The Crawfish Capitol of the World."

Come for crawfish served any way you can imagine: boiled, fried, etouffee, dogs, jambalaya, boudin, pies, bisque, gumbo, et cetera. But make sure you stick around for the Crawfish Races and the Crawfish Eating Contest. The winning crustacean of the race is always mounted for posterity. As for the eating contest, a local lard-butt recently put away 55¾ pounds in forty-five minutes. Other draws include cooking contests, rural crafts, fiddle and accordion music (Wayne Toups is a regular attraction), a dance contest, and the crowning of the Crawfish Royalty. The cost is five clams per day, or $10 for a three-day pass.

For more information, call 318/332-6655.

Bonnie & Clyde Festival

After a two-year crime spree that left twelve people dead, Bonnie Parker and Clyde Barrow etched a place in history for themselves as America's most notorious criminal couple. Their run from the law ended on May 23, 1934, on Ringgold Road, eight miles from the rural parish of Louisiana known as Gibsland. Having stopped to help a farmer with a flat tire, Bonnie and Clyde were mowed down in their car by a whirlwind of bullets spraying from a copse of trees at the side of the road. This historic scene was burned into the American psyche in 1967 when Arthur Penn's movie *Bonnie and Clyde* was released. And now the town of Gibsland brings that same gruesome ambush back to life (and death) every year at the world's only Bonnie & Clyde Festival. A group of actors from Denton, Texas, a town whose local bank was robbed twice by the dynamic duo, show up annually to reenact the scene with blazing guns and lots of fake blood. The actors who play Bonnie and Clyde even drive the real Swiss-cheesed Ford used in the movie.

But that's not all there is to see and hear at this two-day event, which is held on the Saturday in May closest to the anniversary of the shooting. Besides several other reenactments (a bank robbery and a hostage scene), tourists can meet some of Bonnie's and Clyde's relatives, such as Clyde's nephew Buddy Barrow and his sister Marie Barrow. Now and then some of Bonnie's kin show up as well. Then there's Boots Hinton, whose father Ted was one of the six lawmen who participated in the ambush. To get a scholarly perspective, anyone attending the event can sit in on the Friday night historians' meeting. What do they talk about? "They come and argue about stuff," says Billie Gene Poland, one of the festival's organizers and the curator of the Authentic Bonnie and Clyde Museum, also in Gibsland. "An argument went on for a long time about whether Bonnie was pregnant when she died. But her mother said she wasn't because she couldn't get pregnant. Things like that."

Because the local museum doesn't have a budget, they depend on donations, which means the pickin's here are pretty slim, because Bonnie and Clyde paraphernalia fetches top dollar on the crime-curio circuit. However, the museum does have original pictures Bonnie and Clyde took of themselves, of places they visited, of the cemetery where they are buried, and of the six men from the ambush. There also are some gun displays and two female mannequins dressed to look like the gangsters. Poland wants me to get one thing straight though: "Our museum is dedicated to the law officers who ended their career," she says.

Outside the museum, there are lots of vendors selling everything from commemorative T-shirts to small swatches of cloth torn from the pants Clyde was wearing when they were gunned down. All the same, Billy Gene says, "We don't do it to honor Bonnie and Clyde. We do it as a reenactment of history. And we let the law officers win at the end of the festival. It's not like we leave [the gangsters] going free or anything." Maybe if they did, it would give the historians something new to think about.

For more information, call 318/263-9444.

Mardi Gras

on't forget the weirdest of the weird, the wildest of the wild: It's the original Mardi Gras celebrated in New Orleans every February through March.

For details call 504/527-6900 or visit www.mardigrasneworleans.com.

Global Halloween Convergence

et the ghoul times roll! Halloween isn't just for Halloween anymore. Recognizing that there are many people throughout the nation who are fans of goblins, spooks and vampires year-round, the Global Halloween Alliance decided they'd host a Halloween event every summer. While still a young event, the Global Halloween Convergence grew from fifty attendees in Salem, Massachusetts, in August 1999 to an expected 150 for their New Orleans event in June of 2000. Come learn creative haunt ideas, sit in on a professional make-up demonstration, peruse Halloween collectibles and hear a lecture on the nature of fear. But the biggest attraction is the tours. You can walk with ghoulish guides who will give door-to-door accounts of the French Quarters' haunted history; explore the legendary St. Louis Cemetery Number One, New Orleans' oldest city of the dead; and saunter through the history of real and fictional vampire sights. General admission to the convergence is $25 and tours are $15 each.

For more information, call 847/328-3605 or visit www.halloweenalliance.com.

Office Olympics

on't forget the annual Office Olympics, held every September. Here a hundred teams of five men and women office employees compete in events like the Water Break Relay, the Office Chair Roll-Off and Toss the Boss (you have to see it to believe it).

For details call 318/221-9696.

MAINE   MINNESOTA
MARYLAND   MISSISSIPPI
MASSACHUSETTS MISSOURI
MICHIGAN   MONTANA

0

MAINE

 Camden ▶

National Toboggan Championships

Toboggans aren't just for schlepping little Johnny down the street anymore. In cold Camden, Maine, every first weekend in February, the townspeople host the National Toboggan Championships, an amateur event begun in 1990. Today it's swelled into a helluva serious affair, and people come from all over the States with their wooden toboggans roped to the roof of their family SUVs. The toboggan chute is located at the Camden Snow Bowl skiing area. One run along this 400-foot-long chute takes about ten seconds; under prime conditions, forty to fifty miles-per-hour speeds aren't uncommon. But plan early, because the 300 racing slots (which cost $24 to $48, depending on which division you choose) fill up fast. Handmade native ash toboggans can be purchased from Camden Toboggan Company for between $265 and $315, depending on length.

For more information, call 207/230-0490.

 Houlton ▶

Moose Stomper's Weekend

For one-stop shopping, you can hit all kinds of wacky events every February at Houlton's Moose Stomper's Weekend. Try your skills at Human Curling, Human Sled Dog Racing, Wiffle Snow Ball and Potato Peeling contests.

For details call 207/532-4216.

Potato Feast Days

The 7,000-person town of Houlton's biggest and oldest (1959) event of the year is the Potato Feast, which occurs the last week in August. While it's packed with various events from fun runs to arts and crafts to livestock exhibits, the most unique are their potato events. First there's the Potato Picking contest, where people are judged by how fast they can pick potatoes from their earthen rows to fill a bucket. "It's the old-fashioned way," says Becky MacIlroy, the secretary at the Chamber of Commerce and a devout potato lover. "Not everyone can achieve greatness here," she says. "It takes a strong back, since it requires a lot of bending and the ability to move fast." But the main event is the Potato Barrel Rolling Contest, which is the traditional method of moving heavy potato-filled barrels. The participants roll a barrel up and down a mound of dirt that has two wooden planks placed on both sides, then they rush it across the finish line. The winner takes home a crisp $150. Not bad for muscling a bunch of spuds. Potato Feast Days is free to the public and annually attracts around 2,000 people.

For more information, call 207/532-4216.

MARYLAND

 Baltimore

Chicken Clucking and Hog Calling Contest

The Chicken Clucking Contest and the Hog Calling Contest occur every June and July, respectively. These are amateurs-only events. All professional human cluckers and hog callers will be carved and eaten.

For details call 410/396-9177.

 Clarksville

Festival of Carving

Although not nearly the size of the World Wildfowl Carving Championships listed below, the Festival of Carving does have many more categories, which include canes and walking sticks, full-size carousel figures, caricatures, human figures, domestic animals and miniatures, to name a few. While these are all wood-carving events, there is also a special other-than-wood category. $5 will get your carved creation entered into this annual October event. For those not handy with their hands, $3 will get you into the showroom.

For more information, call 301/854-0067.

Antique Valentine Exhibit

If you've got nothing to do the first weekend in February, you should still avoid the Antique Valentine Exhibit, where nineteenth-century valentines and V-Day memorabilia are displayed every year. Please, who cares?

If you want to heckle the organizers, call 301/868-1121.

World Wildfowl Carving Championships

Maryland must be the carving capital of the world. Over 20,000 bird-brained folks have turned out every year for the Ward World Wildfowl Carving Competition since its inception in 1971. For three days every April, some 2,000 carvers of wooden birds put their skills on the line hoping to win first place cash prizes that range from $3,500 to $20,000, depending on what category and what level they are entered in. The three competition levels are Open, Intermediate and Novice. Some categories include Decorative Lifesize Wildfowl, Decorative Lifesize Waterfowl, Decorative Miniature Wildfowl and Interpretive Wood Sculpture. Bird species range from ducks to flamingos to turkeys to eagles to pelicans to hummingbirds. Carvers and spectators alike can take part in various seminars on the art of carving birds. But be forewarned, at $150 each, they are a little pricey. The entry fee is only $8, which is well worth it for a glimpse into this strange world. Ward also hosts the World Fish Carving Competition the same weekend.

For more information, call 410/742-4988 or visit www.wardworld.net.

MASSACHUSETTS

 Boston

Bicycle Messenger World Championships

Every September since 1993, hundreds of bike messengers from twenty-plus countries have met in a pre-designated city (Berlin, San Francisco, London and Washington, D.C., to name a few) to compete in various messengering competitions. The Labor Day event will take place in Boston in the year 2000 and the 2001 event will most likely be held in New York City, though that could not be confirmed at press time. "The biggest event is the main race," says Joel Metz, a San Francisco–based messenger and volunteer organizer. "It's a normal bike race, except there's package delivery and pick-up and other messenger-related things going on." Other events include Cargo (large packages), the Bunny Hop (tricks) and Sprints (speed).

Close to 700 messengers show up every year, paying $40 for registration. Some 2,000 spectators both cheer and jeer the racers and have the added opportunity to stroll through bike-messenger-art exhibits, watch films by and about bike messengers (this new genre of film is presently taking the industry by storm) and listen to music played by, you guessed it, bike messengers. At $20 for a weekend pass, it's a deal. "We try to keep everything as cheap as possible," says Metz. "Messengers and their friends are notorious for not being the most solvent of people." Neophytes can also take a class: How to Become a Bike Messenger. Wouldn't Mama be proud!

For more information, call 415/346-5435 or visit www.messengers.org.

Eastern Naturist Gathering

While clothing-optional gatherings occur all year round all around the United States, the Eastern Naturist Gathering is the big daddy of them all. Although the dates and the locations have changed somewhat over the years, for the last several years it has taken place in Lenox, Massachusetts, during the last week of June. Hundreds of people from every profession and background imaginable show up to shed their clothes and enjoy life as Adam and Eve did in the garden. But don't bet on too much sin here. It's just a bunch of fun-time frolicking in the buff, mixed with lots of social and educational seminars ranging from photography to Native American culture to home beer brewing to massage instruction. Sports include "canuding" (nude canoeing), archery, skeet shooting, and, of course, skinny-dipping. In 1998 they pulled off the World's Largest Nude Frisbee Toss.

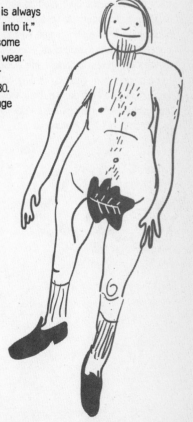

Spokesperson Judi Ditzler stresses clothing is always optional. "Some newcomers choose to ease into it," she says. "And there are often times when some clothing is welcome. For example, one might wear tennis shoes to play tennis." Registration for members is $20 and for nonmembers it's $30. Accommodations with all meals included range from $32 per person per day to $77.50 per person per day for a nice hotel room.

For more information, call 920/426-5009 or visit www.naturistsociety.com.

Rathkamp Matchcover Society Convention

I collected matchbooks when I was a kid, which fueled my passion for burning summer grass in my Texas neighborhood. I'd light the grass on fire and quickly stamp it out. When a fire got out of control one day and burned not only the entire yard but also torched my next door neighbor's grand kid's fort, I was no longer a matchbook collector; I was a pyromaniac. But many people around the world never burned a fort (or at least never got caught) and have continued collecting matchbooks. Many belong to the Rathkamp Matchcover Society, which now boasts a membership of over 10,000. (Dues are $17 for the first year and $14 for every year thereafter.)

Every August, the society holds a convention sponsored by a local club in the town of choice. The 2001 event is scheduled for Indian Wells, California. The usual attendance is about 400 collectors and their families. The event is open to the public for a charge of between $8 and $10. Attendees can expect exhibits of rare matchcovers and matchboxes, auctions, a banquet and a freebie table of donated matchcovers. Event organizer Joe DeGennaro says that matchbook collecting used to be a real "mom-and-pop" hobby. "But now, with Bic lighters everywhere and with smoking on the decline, matchcovers are getting rarer and rarer. Anytime 'rare' comes into the picture, so does money." DeGennaro boasts a "moderate collection of 100,000 matchcovers."

**For more information call
212/876-1730 or visit
www.matchcover.org.**

Fantasia Festival

Whether you're straight, gay, bi-sexual or just your average people-watcher who likes a rip-roaring week-long party in the streets, the annual Fantasia Festival in August has your name on it. Provincetown, an old whaling community at the tip of Cape Cod, has always attracted people with a passion for life. Tennessee Williams wrote *The Glass Menagerie* here in the early forties. Modern artists like Jackson Pollock and Mark Rothko once downed an ocean's worth of cocktails in the local inns and taverns. Today, during the high summer season, it's not unusual to see famous writers like Norman Mailer or celebrated filmmakers like John Waters taking advantage of the gorgeous summer scene.

For the better part of the last quarter century, the Provincetown Business Guild has thrown Fantasia to promote gay and lesbian tourism in the area. With over fourteen week-long events, you could compare Fantasia to a twisted Mardi Gras— a similar street party, but one with more masculine make-up, hairy legs in high heels, gratuitous groping and men and women waving rainbow-colored flags.

Drag Bingo kicks off the event on Wednesday night. And it's just what it sounds like. Over 350 decked-out divas descend upon the Unitarian Universalist Church to try their hand at winning some dough to blow at the opening ball, which occurs immediately afterward. Besides being a knock-down party, the opening ball is the night the queen and king of Fantasia are chosen. Steve Melamed, who owns several local cabarets and is senior co-chair of the Fantasia Committee, explains, "It's primarily attire-based, because there's time limitations and there's sometimes as many as forty to fifty contestants, and we try to do it in two hours." Those vying for crowns also sing, dance and do whatever they must do to get noticed. "But for all practical purposes," Melamed says, "there's no talent to speak of involved. It's strictly costuming."

Costumes are usually designed with no cross-dressing code in mind, though each year does have a theme, such as "Games People Play," "Your Favorite Decade," or "Plays and Movies." "You can really take it as far as you want to take it," Melamed says. "The amount of creativity flowing through here during the week is amazing." One of Melamed's fondest memories is of Miss Bubbles, a cross-dresser who made an elegant gown out of bubble wrap. With the newly appointed king and queen in the lead, Thursday's parade sees thirty to forty floats pass through the streets. Some of the floats are extremely elaborate, some consist of one individual strutting his or her stuff down Electric Avenue. "Last year there was a *Wheel of Fortune* float," Melamed says. "They were using an actual person as the pointer on the wheel." Saucy, to say the least! Tickets are $5 to $10 for individual events; $20 for a weeklong pass.

For more information, call 508/487-2313.

MICHIGAN

Battle Creek

World's Largest Breakfast Table

Every second Saturday in June since 1956, as a part of the Kellogg Company's Golden Jubilee, breakfast is served at the World's Largest Breakfast Table, where upwards of 60,000 (it grows every year) people are served Fruity Pebbles, Pop-Tarts and Tang by 600 volunteer waiters and waitresses.

For details call 616/962-8400.

Farmington

Left-Hander's Festival

The only Left-Hander's Festival in America was sponsored for the first time in August of 1999 by Jeff Goldsmith of Left Hand Publishing. Goldsmith is unsure whether future festivals will be held during the month of August.

For details call 800/511-5338.

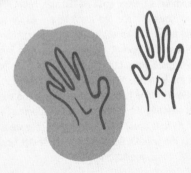

National Baby Food Festival

Ever wondered what baby food tastes like? If you don't have children, you probably haven't tasted it since you were a toddler yourself. Chances are, even those of you who do have children haven't tasted what you stuff into your little Johnny's mouth every day. Here's your chance... The National Baby Food Festival held every year in July—in the hometown of Gerber, no less. Adults can compete in the Baby-Food-Eating Contest, where a team of two, who are connected by a bib, must simultaneously feed each other five jars of baby food with the least amount of spillage. Then there's the Baby Food Cook-Off, where adult chefs must use at least one item of baby food in each of their recipes. But don't leave the kids at home. This baby festival is for babies, too. If yours is a speed demon, enter him or her in the Baby Crawl. While the festival is generally free, some events, like the Baby Crawl ($2) and live musical entertainment ($9 to $15) are not.

**For more information call 800/592-BABY or
visit www.fremont.chamcom.org/bff.html.**

Pyrotechnics Guild International Convention

Every year since 1972, the PGI has held a convention for amateur and professional fireworks enthusiasts of all ages. With a membership of over 3,000, this annual August event proves to be the biggest gathering of fireworks freaks in the country. Their undying energy for grand explosions and flashing colors is evident in their public displays occurring nightly, which beat the hell out of any country-club or public-park shows you've ever witnessed. While the public is invited to the evening shows (for $5 to $10), you must be a member of PGI to enter the convention.

A PGI membership can be obtained by visiting their Website (listed below). Membership is $50 for the first year and $25 for the second and subsequent years. Convention registration for members is $100, plus $20 for each additional household member over the age of eighteen. If you are a member, inside you can expect meetings that feature lectures, seminars, demonstrations, film and video presentations, plus lots of fireworks shooting, including testing of retail class "C" fireworks. Attendees also have a chance to show off at various pyrotechnic competitions. But don't expect Muskegon to host this event every year. The PGI Convention is a roving affair. The event for 2001 is scheduled for Appleton, Wisconsin.

For more information, call 410/655-8594 or visit www.psi.org.

Sault Saint Marie

Snowman Burning

To celebrate the coming of spring, every March since 1971 this small, frozen town makes a little heat for themselves at the Snowman Burning. At this event they torch a ten-foot-tall, 5-foot wide snowman.

For details call 906/635-2314.

MINNESOTA

Austin

Spam Jam

While this isn't quite as fun as Spamarama (see page 182), Austin, Minnesota hosts a nice family-oriented event every July that also celebrates Spam, in the home of Hormel (maker of Spam), no less. That means you get to witness the largest collection of Spam lovers ever assembled. Bring out the bombs! The events are all regular boring festival stuff like softball games, treasure hunts, relay races and fishing contests, plus lots of singing by local artists such as the Spammettes. No event costs more than about $5 to enter and watching is always free. But most importantly, you can sample some pretty amazing grub for about $2 a pop. Just thinking about the food makes my mouth water: Spam Kabobs, Spam Tostados, Spam Nachos, Spam Spring Rolls, Spam Pizza and the list goes on and on because Spam is America's mystery meat. No one knows what's in it, but damn, it eats good.

For more information, call 507/437-3448.

Judy Garland Festival

Born in Grand Rapids, Frances Ethel Gumm is the town's most famous resident. Who is that? Why it's jumping Judy Garland (thank the Lord she changed her name), of course, famed red-slippered star of The *Wizard of Oz*. Since 1975 Grand Rapids has been cashing in on her fame with a June festival full of authors and scholars discussing Garland's life and career, a screening of this famous film, collectors and vendors peddling their wares, plus a gala dinner with a silent auction of various Garland and Oz memorabilia. Featured guests have recently included Munchkins like Sleepyhead Margaret Pellgrini, Coroner Meinhardt Raabe, Lollipop Kid Jerry Marin, plus Garland's daughter Lorna Luft, author of *Me and My Shadows: A Family Memoir*. On your downtime, take a tour of Garland's birth home. Bring you heart, but leave your brain at home.

For more information, call 800/664-JUDY or visit www.judygarland.com.

4'2" TALL. 6'7" WITH THE FLOWERPOT

JACKY CARLSON

Little People of America National Convention

You can call them little people, dwarfs and those short-of-stature, but don't call them midgets, munchkins, pip-squeaks or shrimps—that is, unless you want a set of dentures forever embedded in your kneecaps. In 1957 the legendary little man Billy Barty put LPs on the map by making a public plea for solidarity, which gave birth to the Little People of America National Convention. Now hundreds of LPs gather every year in various places around America to greet, meet, dance, play sports and yes, look for love. Also on hand every year is the Dwarf Expo, which displays products for our vertically challenged friends, such as adaptive driving equipment, clothes, furniture, books, et cetera—things most people take for granted. There are also counseling seminars available. Both dwarfs and nondwarfs of all ages are welcome. Remember that this is an annual traveling convention, so be sure to inquire about future locations for this July event.

For more information, call 402/896-6831 or visit www.lpaonline.org.

Ugly Truck Contest

If you own a shit box, a really rusted out truck that has been wrecked too many times yet can still travel by motor power, you might have a shot at Pelican Rapids' Ugly Truck Contest. With only about twelve entries every July, you have an even better shot at winning the $100 prize. Organizer Len Zierke says, "Trucks are often trailered in, but they still have to be street licensed."

For details call 218/863-6693.

Minnesota Inventor's Congress

his is billed as "The Worlds' Oldest Annual Invention Convention." Every June since 1957, both well-patented and amateur idea men and women have gathered to display their working models or prototypes to would-be investors, manufacturers, marketers and the general public. These men and women are the inventor equivalent to independent filmmakers trying to cash-in on a *Blair Witch Project* blockbuster. Recent inventions on exhibition have been the Soft Touch Mouse, a computer mouse that is activated by the foot; the LPFIS, a liquid-propane-fueled engine for vans and trucks; and the Sport Rebounder, which helps kids practice sports like soccer. A weekend pass for the public goes for $10. Daily rates are $5.

For more information call 800/INVENT1 or visit www.Invent1.org.

Viola

Gopher Count

oila! No, it's Viola, Minnesota, and there ain't no magic here, though the ghosts of millions of huggable little gophers may very well be haunting the fields around this farming community looking for their legs. Legs? In the heart of the Gopher State, the sub-one hundred-person village of Viola has been plagued by galling gophers since local farmers first settled here in the mid-1800s. Not only can a gopher mound really screw up farming equipment, but the little buggers have eating habits that can mean the cancellation of crops. Marilyn Shea, the 1999 Gopher Queen, explains, "They'd go down the rows and eat up all the little corn kernels and alfalfa seeds that the farmers planted. And they just couldn't get a good crop."

So, like any good Americans would do, Violans put a bounty on gophers' legs and started slaughtering the sons of bitches. Their fuzzy front digits are worth cold hard cash, about $1.25 a pair, which is dished out at the annual Gopher Count celebration held every June. How are they stored until this fateful summer day?

Queen Shea explains: "People sometimes stick the legs in a jar and keep them in their freezer until the counting. But some also put them on a line and hang them out to dry. That way they won't smell and the cats won't run off with them from the garage." In 1999 the village paid out almost $1,500, which translates into about 1,200 goner gophers.

It comes as no surprise that, as of late, the Gopher Count has been targeted by animal rights' organizations. Shea, like all Violans, thinks the outside world just doesn't understand. "We don't, you know, trap gophers here to be cruel to animals. And we're not teaching our kids violence. It was something that was started a long time ago, and we keep it going through thick and thin." Ah, good old tradition, the global excuse.

For more information, call 507/876-2439.

MISSISSIPPI

National Anvil Shooting Contest

Even in this book, it's going too far to call anvil shooting a sport, but Gene Mulloy, an old-time blacksmithing buff and co-founder of the World Anvil Shooting Society definitely disagrees. You see, in 1994 he organized the first anvil-shooting competition in the nation, which has become an annual event at Laurel's Wood Expo, held every April. "Anvil shooting dates back to the Civil War," he says, "when all them damn Yanks came through the South destroying all of our metal-working capabilities. They'd put powder underneath the anvils and try to blow them up. And up they went, up in the air." Now a small group of explosion enthusiasts from Mississippi and area states gather to compete for bragging rights in the South.

The rules are simple: a Shooter's anvil must be made of steel, weigh at least one hundred pounds and no more than two pounds of black powder can be used to send that thing soaring. Two classes exist, those who shoot traditional and those who shoot super modified. In the traditional class, shooters use real antique anvils. At the base of every anvil there is a hollow spot, where powder and a ninety-second cannon fuse are packed. Then a second anvil is placed on top of the first. Once the fuse is ignited, the shooter has to haul ass to make it out of the 300-foot danger zone. "The first time I shot, it went about two feet high," Mulloy admits. While anvils shot the traditional way now reach heights up to one hundred feet, for some that just wasn't high enough—hence the humble beginnings of the super-modified category. Not only can shooters in this class smith their own specialty anvils, but they are shot from heavy base-plates that enhance height and accuracy.

In the beginning, Mulloy had trouble deciding how to measure height. "The first year we tried tying a fishing line from a rod and reel to the anvil," he says. "But it just blew that thing all to heck." Then he got a little more sophisticated and had some local mathematicians clock the air-time. Now he uses surveying equipment that offers even more precise readings. Shots are also judged for accuracy, which is measured by how far away from the launchpad the anvil lands. As odd as it seems, no one has ever been crushed by a falling anvil and no one has ever lost an arm to explosives.

While Mulloy calls himself the number one anvil shooter in America, he doesn't hold the world record. You can say it's a sore spot. The world record—held by rival Mike Stringer—is just over 400 feet. In fact, the competition is so heated between these two that Mulloy recently played a cruel trick on Stringer. He built an illegal aluminum-alloy anvil that he shot over 800 feet. "His reaction was gorgeous," Mulloy says. "It was priceless. And we got it all on video. It still rubs him raw when I tell him I have the world record." Admission to the expo is $2.

For more information, call 601/428-0541.

MISSOURI

National Fence Painting Contest

Held since 1956 during the long weekend on or around the Fourth of July, this is the official celebration of Mark Twain, a Missouri native, and his creation, that restless little bugger, Tom Sawyer. The cornerstone of the National Tom Sawyer Days is the National Fence Painting Contest, which is now sanctioned by the U.S. Congress. Many states around the nation hold local fence-painting competitions throughout the year and send their winners to Hannibal for what's known as the World Series of Whitewashing. Since 1964 the travel tab for the winning contestants from ten neighboring states has been picked up by the Jaycees; other state's entries have to pay their own way.

Ten to thirteen-year-old Tom Sawyers are judged on costume, their painting speed and their painting accuracy. A $500 savings bond, prizes donated by local merchants and a trophy, which the winner must present to the governor of his home state, are awarded every year. For all you over-the-hill Tom Sawyers, there's an adult fence-painting contest as well. Another event is the very competitive Tom and Becky Contest, which is open only to Hannibal middle schoolers. Semi-finalist look-alikes must pass two exams—one on Mark Twain and one on Hannibal—and get through a fifteen-minute interview. Throughout the year ten finalists must make appearances locally for the Chamber of Commerce. We're talking upwards of 500 shows! No one ever said being a Tom or a Becky was easy. There are many other contests and games throughout the weekend, such as the Tomboy Sawyer Contest. Hannibal is soooo PC! This event is for all the Martha Dumptrucks of the world. The admission price is $1 per day.

For more information, call 573/221-5052.

Emmett Kelly Clown Festival

Every, final weekend in April, ho-hum Houston, Missouri, gets white-faced and rosy-cheeked celebrating the life of the world famous "Weary Willie." Although many American towns claim Emmett Kelly, Senior as their own, Houston is the only hamlet he ever really called home. Whether you're a class clown or a performing professional, all are welcome to don a bright red wig and floppy shoes and perform in the parade. While the event itself is free, admittance to clown college will cost you $25. Here you'll learn the arts of make-up, juggling, magic, and just plain old clowning around.

For more information, call 417/967-3315.

International Barbershop Quartet Convention

Against all odds, barbershopping is back. In 809 chapters in the United States and Canada, the national organization, The Society for the Preservation and Encouragement of Barbershop Quartet-Singing in America, is almost 35,000 members strong. That's right, an army of sing-songy men with close-cropped beards, wearing styrofoam hats and candy-striped jackets. While this annual Fourth of July event takes place in Kansas City, Missouri, in the year 2000, coming years will be held in Nashville, Tennessee (2001) and Portland, Oregon (2002).

What to expect if you go? Well, a whole helluva lot of singing, of course, impromptu harmonies in line for the urinal, on street corners in town and on stage, where fifty quartets and twenty-five choruses compete every year. There are also plenty of other shows, plus workshops, seminars and clinics. If you're lucky, honorary member Dick Van Dyke will show up with his quartet to do several numbers. But event organizer Reed Sampson says, "The most wonderful thing you will witness is the diversity of our members, men or all ages, from nine to ninety, occupations and ethnic origins, the common thread being the love of four-part a cappella singing." Just mention songs like "Coney Island Baby," "Sweet Adeline" and "Heart of My Heart" to a barbershopper and he'll weep tears of joy. Admission price is $85 for adults and $42.50 for children under twelve.

For more information call 800/876-7464, extension 8592 or visit www.spebsqsa.org.

Typewriter Toss

Don't miss the Typewriter Toss, held annually on April 22, Secretaries Day. Sponsored by local radio station KGBX, this event celebrates frustrated pencil pushers, who—with the help of a lift truck—chunk their old Underwoods from a height of fifty feet. The goal? Besides a killer breakup, it's to hit the bull's eye painted below.

For details call 417/869-1059.

Pub Dart Tournament

Every April local bar and live music venue Blueberry Hill sponsors the oldest (1972) and largest (500 contestants) pub dart tournament in the nation.

For details call 314/727-0880.

MONTANA

Bozeman

Dirt Bag Day

Every March the Big Sky Ski and Summer Resort sponsors Dirt Bag Day, which gives locals and tourists alike the chance to dress up in their nastiest get-ups and parade around the ski slopes. That evening the fun continues at the Dirt Bag Ball, which features live music and the annual crowning of the Dirt Bag King and Queen. Tickets for the party are $10.

For details call 406/995-5886

Clinton

Testicle Festival

Montana tendergroin...cowboy caviar...critter fritters. Come have a ball, or two, or two dozen at Montana's original Testicle Festival. This all-out, five-day fest is held every September at the Rock Creek Lodge, a seedy bunkhouse, bar and casino in the no-man's-land located half-way between Glacier and Yellowstone national parks. The festival is the brainchild of Rod Lincoln, owner of the lodge. Like every year after the festival, he's got a wicked case of laryngitis. "I believe every place should have a signature event that sets it apart. And since there are a lot of Rocky Mountain Oyster thieves around these parts, it was a natural." Then Lincoln adds, "And I just loved the way Testicle Festival rolled off my tongue."

What started out in 1982 as a quirky culinary celebration of Rocky Mountain Oysters (bull balls) for 300 has turned into a 15,000-person, R-rated, knock-em-down, drag-em-out party. "Yep, there's lots of gratuitous nudity, so this is no place for kids. But it's all spontaneous. I guess people are expressing their

First Amendment rights." He's talking about events like the Body Painting Contest, the Co-Ed Naked Pool Tournament, the Wet T-shirt Contest (if T-shirts are worn at all) and the Hairy Chest Contest, where men often drop their drawers to further impress the judges.

There are also events for the clothed, such as Bullshit Bingo, where people buy a square on a huge grid for $5. Every time the bull shits, somebody wins $100. For the thousands of Harley riders who show up every year, there's the Biker Ball-Biting Contest. Lincoln explains, "It's a fishing pole kind of affair. We put a Rocky Mountain Oyster on a clip attached to a line hanging over the street. And girls on the back of a bike try to bite the ball as they pass without using their hands." Other entertainment? Lincoln invited the Seattle Cossacks Motorcycle Stunt and Drill Team to thrill the crowd in 1999. And what party would be complete without lots of music and booze?

But the balls are always the main attraction...the edible kind, that is. In 1999 Lincoln served over 54,000 pounds of USDA-approved Rocky Mountain Oysters quadruple-dipped in a wet-and-dry batter with special herbs and spices. Lincoln laughs, "I like to say Colonel Sanders went to his grave without my recipe." Although the entire event has been free in year's past, in 2000 there will be a $10-per-head charge, whether you stay for a day or for the entire festival.

For more information, call 406/825-4868 or visit www.testyfesty.com.

Cowboy Poetry Gathering

egun in 1986, this is the oldest gathering of cowboy poets in the nation. Every August somewhere in the range of 150 spur-wearing bards with hip-holsters come to Lewistown from around the world to peddle their poems to a crowd of 3,000. Bet you've never met a ten-gallon-hat-wearing Aussie. No, they don't ride kangaroos. But you can come ride on the wit and wisdom of these western wordsmiths. Or why not learn to be a cowboy poet yourself? For $10, workshops are available—shit kickers and handlebar mustaches not included. Also held during the weekend are the Western Art and Cowboy Gear shows. And for those with a hole in their stomach from a hard day of makin' bacon with goats, you can board the Charlie Russell Chew-Choo for a special 3.5 hour dinner train adventure tour, which includes a full-course prime-rib meal, live entertainment and a Wild West train robbery and shoot-out. While the chew-choo costs a whopping $75 per person, the poetry gathering will only run you $5.

For more information, call 406/538-5436 or visit www.lewistownchamber.com

World Famous Bucking Horse Sale

For more than thirty years, Miles City has hosted the world's most prestigious bucking horse sale, part of their Miles City Roundup held every May. Every year top rodeo contractors file in by the hordes to get a glance at over 200 of the newest and wildest broncos on the market. Professional riders attempt to hang on while the feistiest untried stock and spoiled saddle horses strut their stuff around the arena. Heated auctions immediately follow each run. Other attractions include gun exhibits, rare coin shows, parimutuel horse racing, plus lots of barbecue and cowpoke jigging in the streets. It's the cowboy equivalent to Mardi Gras.

For more information, call 406/232-2890.

National Finals Ski-Joring Races

Ski-Joring, a winter event, is a mountain-town tradition. It's a hybrid sport, where a horse and rider pull a skier through a course consisting of about fifteen gates and four jumps. Needless to say, skiers must be pretty brainy on their boards. Wipeouts and collisions are inevitable. The national finals, held every March in Red Lodge, consist of four divisions: Open (teams), Women, Junior, and Longest Jump. The total purse for the weekend is $15,000; registration fees range from $25 for the Junior Division and $100 for the Open.

For more information, call 888/406-3232 or visit www.redlodge.com/ski-joring.

Big Mountain Furniture Race

Leave it to a small, laid-back bunch of snow-blind stoners to put a couch on a pair of old Rossis and ride that honker down the hill. That's what a couple of bored ski patrollers did about thirty years ago. Little did they know that their high-altitude antics would evolve into one of America's most off-the-wall events.

Every April since 1970 the Whitefish Ski Resort has celebrated the end of the ski season with a big blowout that leaves living rooms all around the area a little bare. We're talking recliners, armoires, toilets, baby cribs, trash cans and even coffins affixed to either skis or snowboards. "The definition of furniture is obviously very loose," says Brian Schott, the Big Mountain spokesperson for the event. "Some people even set up living-room scenes where you'll have a couch, a side table, a La-Z Boy and a coffee table with beers and a pizza box on it."

The rules? Well, there aren't too many. Every contestant, of which there are usually about forty, gets one run, must wear a helmet and must have a brake on their craft that functions properly. Judges award points for appearance, speed and accuracy.

NOW, THAT'S A QUICK CRAPPER

KATHY SULLIVAN

This late category is where a good brake comes in handy. At the end of the run is a target, and contestants are scored by how close they can stop without touching it. "You have individuals going for speed, but you also have groups like the local brewery that piles twenty people onto their contraption," Schott says.

The grand prize is a $500 leather recliner donated from a local furniture store. "What usually happens," Schott says, "is that at the end of the race, the party moves to Bier Stube, a local bar here in the village. A lot of the time the winner will auction off the recliner to the highest bidder and get the cash for it." But can just anyone race? Hell yes! Besides the hefty $50 entry fee, you just have to have a killer craft capable of sailing down the snowy mountain. But plan ahead, because word is that local hotels tired of getting cleaned out have started bolting their furniture to the floor.

For more information, call 406/862-1955 or visit www.bigmtn.com.

NEBRASKA NEW MEXICO
NEVADA NEW YORK
HAMPSHIRE NORTH CAROLINA
NEW JERSEY NORTH DAKOTA

NEBRASKA

Ainsworth

Middle of Nowhere Celebration

This one takes the cake for the saddest excuse for a gathering. Every June the poor people of Ainsworth celebrate their boring lives in the "Middle of Nowhere" with wacky events such as a fashion show for five-year-olds, a parade and fireworks. Truly incredible! Yet, it gets even more depressing...the town's nickname came from Walter Ray Williams, a pro bowler who mentioned on national television that he was traveling to the "Middle of Nowhere" for the World Horseshoe Tournament, which the town hosted in 1986. Get a life, Ainsworth!

For more information, call 402/387-2740.

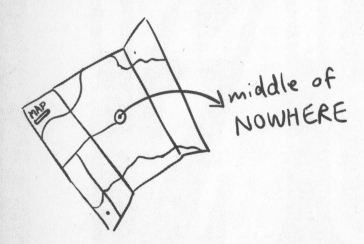

Grandpa John's Amazing Maze

It seems there's a global crew of oddballs who search out and visit mazes around the world. Since 1995 Grandpa John's Amazing Maze in Lincoln has ranked high on their list. Each year before the fall corn harvest, the fifty-one-year-old farmer Grandpa John maps out intricate mazes on graph paper and then puts his skills maneuvering a riding lawn mower to work. And each year the maze is different. The 1999 maze was his most impressive yet, a Star Wars–inspired starship cut into five acres of his cornfield. "The process takes months," Grandpa's wife Judy says. "Then he goes up in an airplane to look it over and take some pictures." A perfectionist, Grandpa always does some more last-minute cutting. Sometimes he even replants some full-grown stalks in areas where he took too much to begin with. From the last weekend in September to Halloween, some 22,000 people pay $5 a head to pass through Grandpa's maze. That equals $110,000, which ain't too bad for several month's work. Sure beats farming, huh Grandpa?

For more information, call 402/470-2450.

Korn Klub Mud Drags

This small town raises revenue with the twice annual (June and September) Korn Klub Mud Drags, where modified cars race in pits of mud.

For details call 402/296-4155.

NEVADA

Burning Man

Black Rock City exists on a 400-mile desert in Nevada. As many as 26,000 people have lived in this town at one time. There are two local newspapers, local radio stations, several churches, libraries, saloons, art galleries, music venues, cafés, barbershops, various barter stores and many other forms of fun, information, culture and commerce—just like in any other town. But this is not any other town. Some even question whether it can really be called a town at all. You see, it's temporary. And money, at least the greenbacks Americans have grown to love, are not welcome here.

THIS JUST MIGHT BE YOUR BOSS

HARROD BLANK

Black Rock City does not exist in any form but in the mind, except during the last couple of weeks of August and the first couple weeks of September.

Every late August since 1990, people have been traveling from all fifty states and many foreign countries to the Black Rock Desert. They bring their own food, their own water, their own shelter and their own contribution, whatever that may be, to Burning Man. It's one of the only events that actually attracts people of every ilk. There are corporate lawyers, hippies, yuppies, hobos, computer programmers, avant-garde artists, drag queens, heavy metal musicians, graphic designers, pyromaniacs, holistic healers, nudists, feminists, motorcycle-gang members, millionaires and the list continues on and on. Even Amazon.com CEO Jeff Bezos is said to be a regular. And here, for about a week, these people come together to create a small world, a small weird drugs-if-you-want-it, don't-need-them-if-you-don't world, for good or evil, though mostly for good.

It's an experiment in temporary community. The rules, well, there really are not many, except that it is "uncool" to interfere with anyone's immediate experience, be that a bad acid trip, a little casual sex with your wife, or a game of desert hockey. And everyone is part of that experience, which means everyone must add to that experience, whether that be with a silly costume or a refrigerated truck for folks to cool off in. Organizer Jim Graham says, "People express themselves in different ways. For the entire event it's the act of giving of yourself. You can give by volunteering as a ranger or a lamplighter, creating a theme camp, doing a performance or wearing a costume."

There are hundreds of theme camps every year. Some are a lot more traditionally useful than others. Some offer free espresso in the mornings, a free book from rows of packed shelves, hardware supplies or sunscreen for when the temperature reaches 107 degrees. Others offer free games of naked croquet, the opportunity to shoot Beanie Babies with paint guns or a different kind of haircut from the Body Hair Barbers. Then there are those camps that are not so easy to explain, but can demonstrate anything—from a new computer capability to a new dimension in artistic expression. The camps themselves are organized in a circle around a 1.5-mile center, where a fifty-two-foot-tall stick-man made of wood and bathed in neon lights awaits burning on the final night of the event; it's a pagan-style celebration that resembles ritualistic worship.

So the final question is: Why? Why not? That's probably the best answer. Burning Man is the brainchild of Larry Harvey, an eccentric former landscaper from San Francisco. The first Burning Man actually occurred on a San Francisco beach in 1986, when Harvey built an eight-foot tall wooden man and burned it for about twenty friends. The rest is history. In a recent speech at Burning Man, Harvey said that the purpose is to combat commodification, or mass production, with individuality. No doubt about it, Burning Man is one of the most individualistic gatherings on this planet. Yet, it's a community as well that does not readily exist in modern society. But don't think this kind of "free" experience won't cost you. You can expect to pay upwards of $200 bucks at the gate to get in, and no tickets are sold at the gate during the final weekend. (Advance tickets are cheaper.) But the roach motel you-can-check-in-but-can't-check-out-until-it's-over rumor is untrue. Graham says, "We discourage (but don't prohibit) day attendance because people who opt for that are selling themselves short of experiencing the sense of community that grows throughout the week."

For more information, call 415/TO-FLAME or visit www.burningman.com.

Las Vegas

Liberace "Play-a-Like" Competition

Needed: Freaks caked in make-up, glitter hairspray, clothes with lots of sequins and shoes like leprechauns. Throw in a little talent at tickling the ivories and you just might have a shot at honoring the memory of one of Vegas's most celebrated performers on his birthday. Held every May, competitors in the Liberace "Play-a-Like" Competition are judged on piano technique, material selection, performance style, with additional credit awarded to those who really deck themselves out *à la Liberace*. There are two categories of competition, the Advanced/Professional and the Amateur/Nonprofessional. Just across the street from Carluccios' Piano Bar (the competition site) is the Liberace Museum Costume Gallery, which is open for praying prior to the event.

For more information, call 818/508-4902.

National Canvention
and Breweriana Show

You read right ... canvention. Beer-can and brew-memorabilia collectors have one heck of a sense of humor, don't they? Since 1975, overgrown frat boys have been meeting every mid-March to exhibit and hawk their wares. For $200 collectors get a room for three nights, a trading table at the canvention center, plus lots of free libations. For $15 the public can get a glimpse inside this strange Bud-on-the-brain world. Even scarier ... find out what floors in what hotels the collectors occupy and pay them a friendly visit. Word is they stay up all night downing suds, trading breweriana and reliving their glory days by building beer-can pyramids.

For more information, call 702/786-1363.

Vegas Ventriloquist Convention

What most people know about ventriloquism they learned at their seventh birthday party. Maybe you remember Bob, the dummy from the television series *Soap*. But there is a burgeoning crew of worldwide vents ranging in age from ten to one hundred who get together every June to celebrate, teach the public and learn about the art of figure manipulation. "There's more demand now for ventriloquists in comedy clubs than there has ever been," says Valentine Vox, who is not only the festival organizer, but a professional vent and the director of Magic & Movie Hall of Fame, which houses the only ventriloquist's museum in the nation.

Just like at any other Vegas attraction, at this convention legends of the industry like Taylor Mason and Dan Horn show off their talents. Throughout the weekend, workshops are held on topics ranging from the basics of comedy writing to making your own figure to using light and sound to improve an act. But the hub of the convention is the dealers' room, where attendees can purchase joke books, scripts, figures and memorabilia. Amateur vents flock to the festival for a chance to be noticed by a talent scout. "We also have a lot of people come who are not ventriloquists," Vox says. "It's a great, fun package. Where else do you get to see and interact with all of ventriloquism's top performers under one roof?" The only kicker is that the price for the entire weekend is $175 for nonmembers, or one-day passes can be purchased for $100.

For more information, call 702/737-1343 or visit www.inquista.com.

Running of the Bulls

Pepe, you're not in Pamplona anymore. Now America has its own Running of the Bulls, thanks to Phil Immordino who staged the first bullish street chase in July of 1998. "It's like Pamplona in that it's bulls running down a road and people running in front of them," Immordino says, "but the bulls are different. The bulls in Spain are trained to kill Matadors. Ours are regular rodeo bulls." Then he laughs. "Now that's not to say a 1,200-pound rodeo bull on your heels isn't scary as hell." For safety there are escape routes every one hundred feet, as well as a six-foot fence, which runners can easily leap over should they feel the breath of a bull. There are also rodeo clowns on hand who are experienced in luring a bull's attention away from runners who just don't cut the mustard.

Immordino hosts four races throughout the weekend, two on Saturday and two on Sunday. He's averaged over 300 runners for each race, pulling in $50 a runner. That translates into a nice little, well, cash cow for Immordino—$60,000 in two days. But the question is: Can you put a price on such ballsy, semi-life-threatening experience? Testimonials on the Website boast, "The rush of my life!" and "I cheated death!" Even if you don't want to run, hell, it's a rush just watching. And that part is free. Over 8,000 spectators show up to cheer on the runners and enjoy live music, food, drink or maybe have a go at a mechanical bull. (Although the Running of the Bulls has been held in Mesquite, Nevada for the last several years, Immordino is looking for a new city to host the event in the spring.)

For more information, call 480/596-5648 or visit www.runwiththebulls.com.

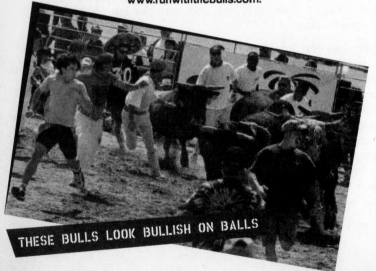

THESE BULLS LOOK BULLISH ON BALLS

International Camel Races

istory has it that in the late 1800s camels were used in the Nevada desert to carry the salt used to reclaim silver and ore. But when the country drooped into a depression, most mining operations were forced to abandon their mines. What did they do with the surplus of their fur-humped friends? The bankrupt operators decided to let them run loose in the desert, where many camels roamed wildly until their American extinction in 1936. But in 1960 camels returned to the desert when Clark Gable, Marilyn Monroe and director John Huston were in Virginia City filming *The Misfits*. The story goes that two newspapers, *The San Francisco Chronicle* and *The Phoenix Sun*, challenged each other to a camel race. Huston, riding for *The Chronicle*, won.

ALL'S WELL EXCEPT FOR THIS HUMP IN MY ASS

JULIA LEE

To celebrate this unique history, Virginia City now imports camels for their annual September race, when an average of twenty-seven jockeys climb on top of these curious creatures and try to get them to run, which isn't always so easy. Camels are known to have short attention spans but can also get pretty crazy, which means sometimes the camels leave their riders in the dust, face first. The race is called "International" because Australians show up every odd year to try to take the crown away from us namby-pamby Americans. While you have to be a pro camel jockey (there was one?) to ride, all you need is $8 to watch. Other events include ostrich races and the rare water-buffalo stampede.

For more information, call 800/200-4557.

NEW HAMPSHIRE

North Conway

Mud Bowl Championships

Since 1975 teams of keg-bellied weekend-warrior football fanatics in the Northeast have been getting together to play some serious ball—some serious mud ball that is. Whether created by rain or an army of sprinklers, teams would get together on fields of mud to prove their civic pride in a game of downright dirty touch football. These are teams with names like the Hampshire Hills Muddas, the Rhode Island Muckaneers, the Merrimack Mudcats and the Mass Mudsharks. In the beginning, the winning championship team would not only get bragging rights, they'd get the honor of hosting the Mud Bowl the following year.

Enter the Mount Valley Washington Hogs from North Conway, who dominated the early years of the sport. In fact, they ended up hosting the championship game so often that they built Hog Coliseum, the only mud-football stadium in the world. Now, every September, the two best mud-football teams duke it out for the mud-football title. But don't go to North Conway just for the game. You have to experience the entire weekend, which begins with Friday night's pep rally, bonfire and drunkfest, which for many slides right into the parade the next morning. At the Mud Parade you'll witness the incredible talents of the New Hampshire Lawnchair Brigade drill team.

For more information, call 603/356-2096.

NEW JERSEY

Quiet Festival

We have a lot of events here all year long," Mark Soifer says, "so I thought we should have a weekend celebrating quiet for a change." The annual Quiet Festival kicks off every November with a "Yawn Along," where upwards of 50 people gather to yawn along to the tune of "Beautiful Dreamer." Other attractions include silent movies, mimes, and the world's only signing choir.

For more info call 609/525-9300.

Weird Contest Week

While this annual August event is different each year, you can expect some mainstays like Taffy Sculpting, French Fry Sculpting, Artistic Pie Eating (boats, seagulls the state of New Jersey), Wet T-shirt Tossing (record: 165 feet), Putrid Puns and Celebrity Super Hero Impersonations. Events occur daily at 11:00 a.m. in front of the Music Pier, boardwalk and Moorlyn Terrace. The grand finale is the highly fashionable Miss Miscellaneous Contest. They've even created a song: "Miss Miscellaneous, so, so spontaneous, never extraneous, even if it would rain on us, it wouldn't be a pain to us, because we adore you, we adore you, Miss Miscellaneous."

For more information, call 609/525-9300.

Miss Miscellaneous

Polar Bear Plunge

roups of old men swimming in icy water, otherwise known as Polar Bear Plunges, are a dime a dozen all around the United States. But nobody pulls one off better than the folks who put on the annual February plunge at Point Pleasant Beach, New Jersey. Begun in 1993 in order to raise money for Special Olympics New Jersey, each plunger must raise at least $100 in order to tiptoe into the thirty-six-degree Atlantic Ocean. The largest Polar Bear Plunge in the world was held in 1998 when 1,200 plungers braved brisk waters, and 100,000 spectators watched them do it. That year over $154,000 was raised for the Special Olympics.

Not only do plungers get a chance to give to a good cause, their registration donation gets them a free sweatshirt and entry for themselves and a guest to the Post Plunge Party, which includes lots of food and entertainment. New Jersey's rival plunge happens every February and also collects donations for the Special Olympics. But this one happens off the beaches of Rehoboth, Delaware, where in 1999 they had almost 1,000 plungers and raised nearly $150,000. Close, but no cigar.

For more information, call 732/213-5387 or visit www.pmx.com/plunge99/info.html.

NEW MEXICO

The National Fiery Foods Show

ot Bitch at the Beach. Kiss Your Ass Good-bye. Widow Maker. Scorned Woman. Witch's Brew. The names of heavy metal garage bands? Hardly, these are just a pinch of the plethora of "Pain is Good"—inspired products on display at the National Fiery Foods Show held every March. Begun in 1988 this is a combination trade and public show. Every year 13,000 people show up, from growers to manufacturers to retailers to Joe fiery food enthusiasts who want to bomb their bellies with products made mainly from habañero peppers. "Some of the most popular products today are in the snack-food arena," says show organizer Dave DeWitt. "We're talking everything from ice cream to cookies to chocolates to hard candy." Some of the more interesting products include quail eggs, vodka, tequila, popcorn and pancake mix. There are also lots of nonfood products such as clothing, books and underwear. "Basically anything with a chili-pepper-emblazoned theme," DeWitt says. There are also cooking demonstrations by noted chefs like Paul Prudhomme and the gumbo-cooking blues band Bill Wharton & The Ingredients. But what's the big draw? "The super-hot sauces continue to be the most controversial," says DeWitt. "These are some of the same active ingredients that are used in the medical field to treat arthritis. And cops spray this stuff on crooks to help restrain them." If you're one of the 13,000 who will pay $7 to cruise around the complex, inquire about how many alarms will be set off by the morsel you're about to throw in your mouth.

For more information, call 505/298-3835 or visit www.fiery-foods.com.

World Shovel Race Championships

Shovel racing is one of the craziest and one of the most exciting new sports in America—for racers and onlookers alike. It was born from the tradition of winter trail-maintenance crews riding their shovels down the mountain after a hard day's work. Now, every February since 1973, the Angel Fire Resort has hosted the championships. Men, women and children compete in two different categories—production and speed-modified—racing down a 1,000-foot course for cash and kudos. Because wipeouts are inevitable, helmets are required.

THE AGONY OF DEFEAT

In the Production Class, contestants ride stock grain-scoop shovels. Riders sit on the shovel, hold their legs in the air on either side of the handle and use their arms for steering. Gail Boles currently holds the Production Record, flying down the hill in 16.66 seconds. That's sixty-seven miles per hour! A Taos native, Boles has only been into shovel racing for about six years. He admits that he didn't get into the sport sooner because it didn't sound like much fun to him. Boles says, "So it was a little bit more exciting than I had initially anticipated." That's an understatement. He was all-out hooked. (While most people bring their own, shovels will be lent to those who don't have one.)

When Production no longer scares you, it's time to try the speed-modified, which Boles describes as "the poor-man's auto racing." These aerodynamic speed machines are built on frames, which are attached to skis or snowboards. A shovel must be incorporated and it must be touching the snow. Boles's craft, attached to a pair of 240-racing skis, is about as high-tech as they come. Designed and built himself, his craft cost him $8,000, an amount he says he's earned back in sponsorships and cash prizes. It incorporates a custom rack and pinion that was made in Detroit, a nitrogen-powered braking system, a chrome molly frame and a durable roll cage. Boles is also a four-time Speed-Modified Champion, the only person to have won in both categories. But he doesn't hold the modified record. His personal best, seventy-eight miles per hour, is just one mile short of the record.

Boles and other Angel Fire-racers, including John Shrader, took shovel racing to the espn2 1997 Winter Extreme Games. But they had a less-than-successful showing because of adverse course conditions. Both Boles and Shrader crashed big time. Shrader broke his back. Boles was knocked unconscious when his machine flipped thirteen times and flew over a wall. While they weren't invited back to the extreme games, highlights of their crashes are still used in extreme games' advertisements. Despite all the pain, both Shrader and Boles are still racing, still perfecting their crafts, still trying to get shovel racing the attention it deserves. Maybe, just maybe, modified shovel racing will become the next addition to the Winter Olympics. The shovel racing is free to watch, but prices for competing run $10 to $70.

For more information, call 505/377-4237 or visit www.angelfireresort.com/shovels.

‹ Carlsbad

International Bat Festival

For six months out of every year, 300,000 Mexican Freetail Bats call the world famous Carlsbad Caverns their home. Every evening for twenty minutes, the sky above the mouth of the cave blackens as the swarm of bats go out to feed. It is estimated that they eat over 3,000 pounds of insects per night. In 1998, employees of Carlsbad Caverns National Park launched the only bat festival in America with the dual intention of "having a lot of fun while teaching the American public more about bats," says Kimberly Carroll, spokesperson for the festival. Now every mid-September park rangers as well as outside professionals give lectures, teach lore, and stage exhibits about bats. The highlight of the weekend is the Sunrise Bat Breakfast, where the public is invited to have a pancake breakfast underneath the bats who return from their midnight bug-athon every a.m. "Nothing like a little guano [bat shit] syrup," Carroll laughs. "No, I'm just kidding," she assures me. What's no joke is that Carroll and the cavern crew have been trying to get one of the many Batman film stars to help promote their festival. "But no luck yet," she says. "We're just a small, batty little town."

For more information, call 505/887-6341.

Whole Enchilada Fiesta

he city of Las Cruces celebrates its heritage every October when local Mexican-food amigo and spice-meister Roberto Estrada cooks (with the help of eleven sous chefs) the World's Largest Enchilada, which measures just over thirty feet in diameter. The ingredients? Try 750 pounds of stone-ground corn, 175 gallons of vegetable oil, 75 gallons of red chili sauce, 50 pounds of chopped onions, and 175 pounds of grated cheese. We're talking major belly ache here. But festivalgoers seem to smile as a piece of local history slides down their gullet. However, if the crowd outside the porta-pots is any sign, the whole enchilada is a lot better going down than keeping down. Every year since 1970, over 70,000 hungry heffers with bullet-proof bellies have polished off the whole enchilada plus enough gorditas, fajitas and tamales to feed Santa Anna's army. Cold Cerveza, mariachi music and the heated annual police department versus fire department boxing match round off the event.

For more information, call 505/524-6832.

 Lovington

World's Greatest Lizard Races

very Fourth of July it's not fireworks that light up the faces of Lovington's little ones. It's their natural need for speed, which is supplied by lightning-quick lizards. At the Chaparral Park Speedway, the world's premier mini-reptile racetrack, lizards of every ilk vie for top honors in a race that has become synonymous with do-or-die competition. The course is the most difficult in the country, featuring a perilous sixteen-foot ramp that feeds into an ominous plexiglass container. But adults beware: Your lizardry isn't wanted here. Only kids under sixteen can enter.

While some gung-ho young guns import only the finest lizards from rival towns and train them year-round, most catch theirs within a week of the race, some the day of. Prior planning isn't necessary as Lovington is a veritable breeding ground for various lizard species, such as the mountain boomer, the horny toad, the gecko and the skink. While that may be true, catching these buggers is a pain in the butt. (Hint: Use a rope-headed mop.) The largest racer to date was an eighteen-inch iguana. Intrigued by the beast, the crowd circled in close. When the starter's pistol exploded, the iguana hopped to his hind legs, flared the loose skin around his head, and made like Godzilla down the track. Needless to say, this unexpected display sent the spectators running. The iguana? Having frozen at the finish line, he didn't even win.

Another interesting moment in race history happened in 1976 at the inaugural race. Before the present-day streamlined track, the race was held in a horse tank. The entrants were caged underneath a tub in the center of the tank, and the crowd pushed and shoved for a front-row spot around the tank, cameras ready. When the tub was finally turned, the lizards did not move. Petrified by the hundreds of faces and flashes, they did what all good lizards do. They began to eat each other. That year the lizard with the biggest stomach took the title.

For more information, call 505/296-2944.

Roswell

UFO Encounter

The military town of Roswell is the home of the famous Roswell Incident. In July of 1947, a flying saucer was rumored to have crashed on a ranch northwest of town. Two nuns on duty at St. Mary's Hospital, a couple enjoying a romantic rendezvous and a ranch foreman named Mae Brazel witnessed the crash. But hushed by the government, what these people saw went unreported, and the crash was not explored until 1970. Some profess this crash proves aliens exist. Some say no way. Both believers and skeptics come together for this annual July event. There's fun for the whole Jetson family here (most of it is free), from an Intergalactic Fashion Show to the Trivia Star Quiz to tours of the International UFO Museum and Research Center to walks around the infamous crash site. And what other-world event would be complete without some *Star Trek* celebrities? Bring it on, Sulu.

For more information, call 505/624-6860 or visit www.roswellufoencounter.com.

Elfego Baca Shoot

This is another all-terrain, guerilla golf match *à la* the Pillar Mountain Classic (see page 7). But the Elfego Baca Shoot is actually the older of the two; it's been held since 1960. And my money goes to this one as being the tougher of the two. Which would you prefer to battle? I think a little cold wind and the chance of breaking your butt slipping on ice is no match for rattlesnakes, scorpions, cactus barbs, biting black gnats and high desert sun mixed with the potential for falling in an abandoned mine shaft and never being heard from again. But that doesn't stop the ten brave souls who participate every year. That's ten maximum, so if you plan to enter, get your registration in early. If you plan to play, here's what to expect at this June tourney.

First you will need three good friends who owe you a big favor. They will be your designated spotters, those who keep an eye on where your ball flies, which you'll realize is a must after watching your tee shot whistle 1,000 yards down the face of the mountain. Each player only gets ten balls to finish and each lost ball adds a stroke to your score, so choose your friends wisely. Equipped with a few old drivers, heavy socks, rugged boots, caps, canteens, walkie-talkies, binos and bug spray, you and your team will mount a four-wheel-drive vehicle that will carry you to the top of the 7,243-foot Socorro Peak. Here begins the longest one-hole golf tournament in the world, a course that descends 2,550 feet and spans about three miles of ultra-sketchy terrain. The payoff for risking your life? $200 in golf gear. In other words, you really have to love the sport. While the scores often range in the seventies (the scorecard goes to seventy-five), Mike Stanley, the reigning champ, shot an impressive nine.

The tournament's name comes from Socorro's infamous Sheriff Elfego Baca, who deputized himself at the age of nineteen to control the desperado population. The story goes that in 1884 Baca was trapped in an adobe hut by a gang of outlaws. After pumping 4,000 rounds of ammunition into the hut, sure that Baca was dead, the desperadoes let down their guard. When the dust had cleared, Baca emerged and single-handedly arrested all of them.

For more information, call 505/835-1550.

NEW YORK

Brooklyn ◄

Nathan's Famous Hot Dog Eating Contest

Don't miss Nathan's Famous Hot Dog Eating Contest held every July fourth at the original Nathan's in Coney Island. Eleven regional champs and four international champs compete to see who can munch the most in twelve minutes. Come see if last year's 130-pound Japanese victor Hirofumi Nakajima, who downed 24.5 dogs, can keep the crown.

For details call 212/627-5766 or visit www.sheacommunications.com.

Buffalo ◄

World's Largest Disco

As the sun began to fall on the seventies, as the world began to turn its back on disco music, in 1979 one last hurrah was held in Buffalo, New York. Gloria Gaynor and The Trammps were on hand singing their anthems of the era, "I Will Survive" and "Disco Inferno." Over 13,000 people showed up to point their fingers to the sky and dance the night away for what they thought would be the last time. That night was entered in *The Guinness Book of World Records* as the largest dance party in history. With

DIGGING ON SUPER 70S WEAR

ELIZABETH ZAKY

the advent of punk and new wave music storming the nation in the eighties, disco records were burned or shunned like leprosy. Although the music may have stopped, it was not forgotten.

In 1994 on the eve of the fifteenth anniversary of the original event, the World's Largest Disco was revived. Again, the Trammps were on hand to sing to a new generation of disco fans. While only 1,800 people showed up, local promoters thought it was a success and have been throwing the party every year since, held the Saturday before Thanksgiving in the Buffalo Convention Center. In 1999 a capacity crowd of 7,000, who each paid $20 to enter, showed up to juke and jive to 72,000 watts of disco under a rainbow of lights. In years past super seventies celebs like Isaac from *The Love Boat*, Greg from *The Brady Bunch*, the Hanson brothers from the movie *Slapshot*, Tabitha from *Bewitched* and *Dance Fever*'s Deney Terrio have been on hand. A painted replica of the *Partridge Family* bus is always parked in front.

About 70 percent of the crowd dresses up every year. "It's kind of like Halloween in November," promoter Dave Pietrowski says. Local formal wear and costume shops stock lots of powder-blue tuxedos, platform shoes and giant afro wigs just for the event. "Those who don't dress up always feel out of place," he says. If you've got a little night fever left in your bones and feel like staying alive, this is the place for you. Dynamite!

For more information, call 716/635-8668 or visit www.worldslargestdisco.com.

New York

24-Hour Marriage Marathon

his ain't no Elvis drive-thru chapel in Vegas. Think bigger, better, taller and cheaper—think top of the world, 110 stories above the city streets, 1,377 feet above the most romantic city in America, New York City. On the observation deck (the highest outdoor observation deck in the world) at the top of the World Trade Center, every Valentine's Day, beginning at 12:01 a.m., the first of fifty-five couples in a twenty-four-hour period are joined in wedded bliss. They are all married in civil ceremony before a New York State Supreme Court Justice in a specially constructed wedding chapel.

Besides nosebleeds and butterflies, all of the lucky newlyweds receive gifts donated by local businesses. No, you won't receive matching sweatshirts or a free eye exam at your nearest Sears Vision Center (though several years down the line you may wish you had that prior to the ceremony), but being a member of the Top of the World Marriage Club has its advantages. You'll be in line to receive a free honeymoon (years past have included Morocco and Jamaica), a $500 shopping spree at Bloomingdale's, Broadway tickets, dinner for two at Windows on the World, a weekend at Gurney's Inn Resort & Spa in Montauk, Long Island, plus many others.

How much does this all cost? Not a penny. All you have to do is submit an application after January 1, which should include an essay stating why you want to get married atop the highest building in New York City. It's that easy. Because the event still being fairly new, its organizers barely fill the fifty-five-slot maximum each year. If you're not looking to get hitched, the normal $6.25 to $12.50 ticket fee for the observation deck is doubly worth it!

For more information, call 212/323-2340.

Westminster Kennel Club Dog Show

I know this might not seem so "off-the-wall" to most, but a dog show that has been around since 1877 deserves at least a mention. And come on, anyone who gets snotty about the breed of their dog is bizarre in my book. Nonetheless, this dog show is second only to the Kentucky Derby as the "oldest continuous" sporting event in America. Over 2,500 dogs are entered to compete for best in their breed, which include sporting dogs, hounds, working dogs and terriers. This is an annual February event, which costs $31 per day or $52 for the entire two-day event.

For more information, check out the club's Website at www.westminsterkennelclub.org.

Wigstock

For another group of puppies who really know how to pounce, come to New York in September for America's wildest transexual-Transylvanian festival extraordinaire. In 1999 some 10,000 perky wig-wearers came out to show their wares in the streets of the city. Every year promises live entertainment from the celebrity drag and porn worlds such as The Lady Chablis from John Berendt's book *Midnight in the Garden of Good and Evil*. While the $20 admission price is pretty steep, the people-watching alone at this daylong gaud-awful affair is worth every penny. Want to test-drive the event? Go to your local video store and see if they have *Wigstock: The Movie*, a documentary made in 1995.

For more information, call 212/691-7198.

Niagara Falls

International Jugglers Festival

Although the International Jugglers Association has been around since the late forties, they didn't start meeting seriously for conventions until the early seventies. Now, over a thousand bowling-pin tossers show up every July to strut their stuff and learn a new trick or two from some industry gods. Jugglers of all ages and all levels of expertise compete both for fun and prizes. Open to the public, entry costs just $2 per day, which will get you into contemporary juggling shows like Airjazz, three juggling dancers who also happen to be National Juggling Champions. Maybe the most enjoyable event is the Numbers Challenge, where attempts are made every year to break *The Guinness Book of World Records* for the maximum number of objects juggled. If you've always wanted to learn to juggle, step right up.

For more information, call 413/367-9398 or visit www.juggle.org.

NORTH CAROLINA

Wooly Worm Festival

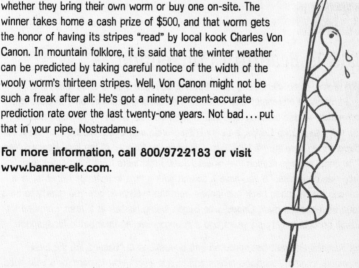

Amid the reds and yellows of autumn, deep in the Blue Ridge Mountains, the 400-person town of Banner Elk becomes a booming metropolis of 25,000 during their annual October Wooly Worm Festival. The main event is the wooly-worm races. The racetrack is on the backboard of a flatbed trailer, where about twenty strings hang from top to bottom. Throughout the day, in about sixty heats, worms inch up the strings, crossing the finish line at astonishing speeds. Anyone can enter for $5, whether they bring their own worm or buy one on-site. The winner takes home a cash prize of $500, and that worm gets the honor of having its stripes "read" by local kook Charles Von Canon. In mountain folklore, it is said that the winter weather can be predicted by taking careful notice of the width of the wooly worm's thirteen stripes. Well, Von Canon might not be such a freak after all: He's got a ninety percent-accurate prediction rate over the last twenty-one years. Not bad ... put that in your pipe, Nostradamus.

For more information, call 800/972-2183 or visit www.banner-elk.com.

Sleazefest

This is a cheesy rock 'n' roll redneck festival held annually in August in several bars in downtown Chapel Hill. It's the brainchild of the band Southern Culture on the Skids, which schedules three days' worth of music, hot Bud in a can, barbecue, Wonder Bread, Cheese Whiz, Snow Balls and an assortment of other trailer-trash surprises. Expect the entire Duke clan, or at least those dressed like them, to show up in full force. If you're lucky, you'll witness the Woggles's on-stage barbecue-sauce baptism of anyone who wants to be saved. Tickets are $20 per night or $55 for the entire event.

For more information, visit www.sleazefest.com.

World Beer Festival

Don't forget Durham's World Beer Festival every October.
For details call 800/977-2337.

Bald Is Beautiful Convention

Chrome-dome alert! Long hairs beware, because skin is in. At least in smallsville Morehead City, home of the annual September Bald Is Beautiful Convention, whose headquarters are located on Bald Street. "Morehead means less hair," says John Capps, a beefy buffed-brain who could pass as the stunt double for an over-the-hill Mr. Clean. Capps is the founder of the Bald Headed Men of America, an organization that boasts 35,000 members from fifty states and thirty-nine countries. "If you have a haircut with a hole in it, fringe benefits, or a forehead that reaches back five inches from the eyebrows, hey, you qualify to be a proud bald-headed man." Capps, who began losing his hair at fifteen, corralled his cueball cohorts twenty-six years ago and began waging their battle for respect.

This September event has sprouted into a weekend of "Baldies are the best!" ceremonial chants, feel-good clinics and advice about how to care for a bald head, such as, "What happens if you shave off little red stubbies that pop up on top of your head?" There are tons o' corny contests, including Sexiest Bald Head, Most-Improved Bald Head, Most-Distinguished Bald Head, not to mention awards for Telly Savalas and Montel Williams look-alikes. But probably the most-impressive aspect of Capps's bald-headed career is that he has perfected the art of hair guessing. He promises that just by speaking with you he'll be able to tell what kind of haircut you're sporting. "I don't miss," Capps grunts. So give him a call. He just might knock your rug off.

For more information, call (252) 726-1855 or visit members.aol.com/baldusa.

Mayberry Days

September 1990 marked the thirtieth anniversary of *The Andy Griffith Show* and the first Mayberry Days celebration in Mount Airy, the birthplace of Andy Griffith. What started as a one-day event with a crowd of 800 has swelled into a three-day celebration of one of America's most memorable television series. Folks from Mayberry drop by every year, though they don't look quite the same anymore. You might see George Lindsay (Goober), Maggie Peterson Mancuso (Charlene) and Richard Linke (the show's producer and Andy's personal manager). Or you might witness the unveiling of the Otis Cambell wardrobe (on loan from the estate of Hal Smith and *The Andy Griffith Show* Rerun-Watchers Club). Or maybe you'll want to stop by the local restaurant Snappy Lunch and try your hand at the Mayberry Days Pork Chop Sandwich-Eating Contest. They should call it Vomit Days. The record is a mere five sandwiches, so the title is up for the taking. The fest is free for all fans. But remember this: Don't breathe a word about Mayberry being a fictitious town, because if you do, a local Andy Griffith look-alike will cuff you, stuff you and dump you naked at the border.

For more information, call 800/286-6193 or visit www.visitmayberry.com.

National Hollerin' Contest

The National Hollerin' Contest gets my vote for the most culturally unique yet odd gathering in America. Hollerin'? Before the Internet, before the telephone, before the CB radio, before the automobile, before the daily newspaper, before just about anything used to project news and sound, people used to holler to get their message heard. Throughout the world, there was a time when hollerin' was the chief means of communication. As champion hollerer H.H. Oliver says, "It was a thing that had to go on. When you had trouble, you had to holler. There was as much a need for hollerin' as there was for eatin' in that day." Some hollered when they were in trouble, others used it to call their cattle, some just did it when they were good and drunk. Whatever the reason, everyone had their signature holler that was as recognizable their own name.

Like many of the events in this book, the National Hollerin' Contest just sort of happened. In 1969 Ermon Godwin, a guest on a local radio show mentioned hollerin'. The host, John Thomas, reacted by telling Godwin that there should be a contest. Much to Godwin's surprise, 5,000 folks turned out that first year. Thirty-some years later, the contest is alive and well and has grown multifold. Besides the hollerin', there are whistling, conch-shell blowing, fox-horn blowing and green-pepper contests. Then there's something called the watermelon roll. In this event contestants attempt to carry a watermelon a distance of twenty yards while a member of the local volunteer fire department tries to knock them off their feet with a high-pressure firehose. While this is an alcohol-free event, you can bet the doublewide that homemade wine and corn whiskey isn't hard to find. Admission to this daylong event in June is $3.

For more information, call 910/567-2600 or for an audio sample of some hollerin' visit www.intrstar.net/~hollerin.

NORTH DAKOTA

Dunseith

International Old-Time Fiddlers Contest

Dunseith, North Dakota, is the place to witness some of the best fiddle playing on the planet. Fiddlers ranging in age from under thirteen to over sixty-five compete in different classes for cash prizes upwards of $400. There is no registration fee to enter this annual June event, which was first held in 1975. But to be one of the 2,000 people who attend every year, you'll need to shell out $7 per day, plus an extra $6 per day if you want to see the evening entertainment. The best deal is to buy a weekend pass for $13, which gives you access to everything.

For more information, call 701/838-8472.

OHIO
OKLAHOMA
OREGON

OHIO

All-American Soap Box Derby

This classic sport has the power to take both participants and spectators back to a simpler time in American history, when little Johnny and little Sue put a milk crate on wheels and raced down a local hill instead of shooting each other. Since 1934 kids of all ages have been making these hill-powered vehicles, pitting themselves against others in small towns across the nation. What started out as a hobby for many has grown into a competitive series, where kids race in locally sanctioned events in order to qualify for the All-American Soap Box Derby, held every August in Akron. This event attracts over 15,000 spectators and about 300 racers, who come from such faraway places as Germany, Venezuela and the Philippines.

Racers compete in three divisions. The Stock Division is for first-time builders who create their cars from kits. The Super-Stock Division is for kids who want to build more advanced models. And the Masters Division is the advanced class, for kids who build crafts that look like mini dragsters without the motors. The track in Akron is a 954-foot straightaway course that is on an eleven percent grade, allowing racers to reach speeds over thirty miles per hour. Although racers compete for free, there is a $5 spectator charge.

For more information, call 330/733-8723 or visit www.aasbd.org.

National Tractor Pulling Championships

If you've never been to a tractor pull, this is the one to hit. Although there are hundreds of tractor pulls all around America, all of them generally the same, this is the biggest, baddest and one of the oldest. Since 1966 farmers in these parts have been souping up their John Deeres in order to see who can pull a huge hunk of steel (a motorized mechanical exchanger) the farthest and fastest. And every August some 60,000 people pay either $15 per session or $60 for a weekend pass to see the best tractor pullers our great country has to offer competing for an overall purse of $150,000.

For more information, visit www.pulltown.com.

Ganesh's Birthday

On March 15, 1998, Ganesh became the first elephant born in Ohio since the Stone Ages when woolly mammoths roamed the area. Now every March the Cincinnati Zoo celebrates Ganesh's Birthday with a giant card, giant cake and afterwards... a bath. Entrance to the zoo ranges between $4.75 and $10, with a $5 charge for parking.

For details call 800/944-4776.

Dandelion Festival

Every first Saturday in May, which just happens to be National Dandelion Day, Breitenbach Wine Cellars hosts the annual Dandelion Festival. Why is a winery hosting a flower festival? Well, for the last twenty years Breitenbach has been making wine completely from dandelions—no grapes. After following the growing interest in the flower for a number of years, in 1993 they decided to kick off a festival that now attracts 20,000 people. Like me, they are all probably surprised to learn that dandelion leaves contain twice as much calcium as spinach, more vitamin A and E than broccoli, and high quantities of iron, riboflavin, and lecithin.

Dandelions are healthy for the bod and the brain. And to give people some helpful hints, there are many different dandelion food products free for tasting, such as dandelion-cheese bread, dandelion gravy, dandelion ice cream and dandelion coffee. "For the coffee," festival organizer Anita Gates says, "they take the dandelion root, roast it and then grind it up." The festival also hosts the National Dandelion Cook-off. Months before the event over a hundred dandelion chefs from around the nation draft up ideas for dandelion delicacies and submit the recipes to the judges. Ten finalists are invited to compete for a cash prize of $500.

For more information, call 800/THE-WINE or visit www.breitenbachwine.com.

Gene Autry Days

Nope, America's favorite Hollywood "Singing Cowboy" wasn't born here. And, no, he didn't die here. In fact, he only visited Kenton once in his life, in 1938. Yet, since the mid-thirties, the folks in this small town have always felt like they've known the man personally. You see, the Kenton Hardware Company, which employed half the town at that time, was quickly moving toward bankruptcy. But they hung on, cutting jobs, until 1936, when they received a contract to produce toy cap guns to be sold as Gene Autry collectibles. That toy soon became the hottest-selling toy in America (records show that over 6 million were manufactured), which not only saved the company, but the town in general.

This is the feel-good entry of the book. Go make yourself feel good by getting your mule to take you to Gene Autry Days to celebrate the "Singing Cowboy," who died in 1998, and the employees of the Kenton Toy Company. Besides lots of western music and entertainment guests—Peter Breck, who starred in *Big Valley* as Nick Barclay showed up in 1999—there is an antique and toy market and the Sullivan Johnson Museum, which has a Kenton Hardware Company display and dozens of cast-iron toys, plus a good representation of Gene Autry collectibles. Staged since 1992, this annual July event is $4 per person per day.

For more information, call 419/673-4131.

Steubenville

Dent National Championships

emolition derby is the fifty-year-old of sport of smashing beat-up cars into each other. Drivers aim for the radiator and wheel panels. The last car running wins. Although many small towns host a national championship, the Dent National Championships, founded in 1998, is the real deal. Driver and Dent rep Todd Dubé says, "We will only allow current feature winners from any derby in the country to enter, but they must show proof." Because the Dent purse is $20,000 ($10,000 to the winner), you can see why some might try to forge their way in. "We have to check up on these guys," Dubé explains, "because they have a tendency to fabricate the proof every now and then." Not only is Dent the biggest derby, averaging over a hundred drivers and upwards of 15,000 spectators, but it's also the baddest. "People are always blown away with how vicious the derby we put on is," Dubé boasts. "It's the hardcore of the sport. We almost had two drivers killed at our last event because of severe hits." While the most recent Dent National

KING OF THE JUNKYARD

DENT PRODUCTIONS, INC.

Championships happened in Steubenville, Ohio, the event changes locations every year. Tickets for the event usually range between $12 and $15, and it always occurs in late April or early May.

For more information, call 716/627-1234 or visit www.dentusa.com.

Twins Days

Which came first, the town or the gathering? In this case, it happens to be the town, which, since 1976, has put its name to good use by holding the world's largest annual gathering of twins. Every August about 3,000 sets of twins descend upon Twinsburg to celebrate their unique genetic structure. Other multiple births such as triplets and quadruplets are welcome as well. Well, anyone is welcome for that matter, and Twin Days attracts more than 60,000 visitors to this three-day-long event. However, it seems like there's a little discrimination going on here: anyone of multiple birth only has to pay $5 for the festival while all single-birth babies have to shell out $10.

For more information, call 330/425-3652 or visit www.twinsdays.org.

OKLAHOMA

World Cow Chip Throwing Championships

Sick of taking crap from assholes? Then get your butt to Beaver, the site of the annual World Cow Chip Throwing Championships. That's right sludge-swallowers, April is the month to pitch a little poop yourself. The event dates back to 1970 when Beaver—like one-horse towns all across America—was having an identity crisis. "We had no pizzazz," says Kirk Fisher, who is one of Cow Chip's founding fathers and is the current emcee. "No one acknowledged us. But after that first fling, people came by the droves to throw those damn things." What started as an off-the-cuff idea has slowly progressed not only into the national, but the international sporting arena. Sport? Although not yet Olympic level, different hoedown hamlets all across the States, plus foreign locales like Japan, Germany and Australia, conduct their own sanctioned contests with hopes that their local far-flinger will return from Beaver with the crown.

WELCOME TO THE SHIT-SLINGER'S BALL

BRENT LANSDEN

Cow chips have been the saving grace in many range communities for hundreds of years. Early settlers depended on the humble commodity to keep them warm during the winter. Because it produces an odorless, sootless heat more intense than local lumber, cow chips fueled many a campfire, stove and indoor furnace—not to mention a baby-making romp or two. Imagine the ambiance! "Honey, I've got a heap o' dung warming in the fire. What do you say we get nasty?" So important was dried shit to the New World that some even go as far as to call it "brown gold";

local literature has it ma and pa used to trade wagon loads for needed food and supplies.

Now cow chips bring a different kind of gold and glory to the local economy. Thirty-five greenbacks insure a shot at world recognition. Every year, a lucky few Beaverites search secret fields for the cream of the crop. "Rules say they have to be local chips no less than six inches in diameter," Fisher says. "The damn Texans always think theirs are better and try to sneak in their own. We've even had to go as far as to post a round-the-clock guard for the chip wagon." Each anxious contestant chooses two chips from the piled-high petrified pancakes. Rules? Well, there's no hard-and-fast tossing technique. "But," Fisher says, "this is a bare-handed ordeal."

Jim Pass, who hails from Plains, Kansas (just forty miles up the highway from Beaver), is the 1998 world champ. Although not a great outing, Jim took home the proverbial cake with a 158-foot-1-inch hurl, well behind the world record 182-foot-3-inch heave by Leland Searcy in 1979. Jim's technique? "I usually pick a chip that's about eight inches across," he says, "one that isn't too wet, but isn't too dry either. And it's got to be fairly flat, and then I just throw it like a baseball." Pass says he grew up in a sports-oriented family, so it wasn't hard for him to master cow-chip trajectory. Holding his chip at the edge with all five fingers, he cocks and releases at a forty-five to fifty degree angle, giving it just a hint of backspin. Although Pass has never practiced before, he says this year might be different. "It's gotten serious now," he says. "I'm going for the world record, so I just might slip out into the yard and try a practice throw or two."

For more information, call 580/625-4726.

McAlester

The World's Only Prison Rodeo

Founded in 1940, the Oklahoma State Prison Rodeo is the world's only rodeo held completely behind prison walls. Normal joes can get a behind-the-scenes glimpse inside a maximum-security correctional facility while watching some real men-in-black teach cows and horses who is king. While watching your back to make sure you don't get shivved makes for an intense rodeo-watching experience, the crowd seems to enjoy it more when the inmates are all on the rodeo floor competing in an event called Money the Hard Way. Every year rodeo organizers let a Brahma bull loose in the arena with a $100 bill tied to one of his horns. Since $100 is worth about four-months' pay to these hardened criminals, be ready for one helluva scrap for that C note. Almost 15,000 spectators show up for this two-night September event. Tickets range from $6 to $15.

For more information, call 918/423-2550.

OREGON

Kinetic Sculpture Races

As a part of Corvalis's annual da Vinci Days Festival, a three-day-long July event that showcases the best in art, science and technology (in the spirit of Leonardo, or course), they have hosted the Kinetic Sculpture Races since 1992. Raan Young approached the festival organizers with the concept after meeting two men who started the first race in Eureka, California, in the late sixties. The vehicles are human-powered all-terrain vehicles. Racers combine artistry and engineering to create vehicles that can travel with equanimity over ten miles of city streets, 100 feet of thick mud, down two miles of the Willamette River, across 3,000 feet of sundried clay and finally over 100 feet of sand. In the past, vehicles have run the spectrum from a functional mountain bike with a rubber flotation device attached to the back to full-blown sculptures on wheels. "Ninety-nine percent of them are pedaled," Young explains. Frames have included elaborate renditions of dragons, warthogs and fish, as well as abstract works of art.

Young's ongoing involvement with kinetic-sculpture racing rests on the notion that it brings together disciplines that normally do not interact, such as art and engineering. "It's also important for kids to see that adults can be crazy and have fun, too," he says. Anyone with a mind to build a vehicle can enter. The cost is $70 for a team of two to enter, which also includes a weekend pass to the festival. Weekend admission for adults is $9, and it's $5 for children; spectators are encouraged to wear costumes to enhance the racing experience for all. Other attractions include a film and video festival, music, theater, trash-can art, science lectures and a world-class kite exhibit.

For more information, call 541/757-6363 or visit www.davinci-days.org.

Betty Picnic

he annual Betty Picnic takes place every June. While you don't need to be named Betty to enter, this event is a celebration of "the Bettys of this world for their vivacity, impulsiveness and similarities."

For details call either Betty Wilder or Betty Patterson, two of the many Bettys who show up every year, 541/476-4104.

St. Urho's Day

estivals celebrating a population's heritage are common. Festivals celebrating Finnish heritage are less common. And a Finnish celebration like Hood River's St. Urho's Day, held every March, is not common at all. In fact, it's a little strange. Legend has it that back in the homeland, Saint Urho recognized that grasshoppers were destroying grape crops. You know what that means, right? Those damn grasshoppers were cutting down on the country's quantity of wine. It's enough to make a Finn go bonkers. So sweet Saint Urho grabbed a pitchfork and successfully banished all of the grasshoppers across the sea and into Ireland.

However, it wasn't until 1981 that Felix Tomlinson noticed Hood River had a large Finnish population—Alajokis, Lingrens, Kestis, Lahtis, et cetera—and organized some of them (three) for the first parade, then quickly retired to the nearest bar. Now a queen is chosen every year and paraded through town in a brightly colored Urho-mobile. Other paraders include the Finnish Drill Team (breasty women holding Black & Deckers that swirl Finnish flags); the Iron Maidens (Viking-clothed vixens holding hockey sticks and wearing horned helmets); and at the front of the crowd (well, the whole shebang, paraders and spectators alike, is only about one hundred people), is Tomlinson himself in his signature lime green polyester leisure suit. If you are one of the folks in the "crowd," lucky you—you get to pelt the paraders with grapes. Good random fun...nowhere else but Oregon.

For more information, call 541/386-5785.

Robin Hood Festival

Just as Metropolis, Illinois, celebrates Superman (see page 69), so too does Sherwood, Oregon, celebrate the legendary man in tights at the annual Robin Hood Festival held every July.

For details call 503/625-6873.

Veneta

Oregon Country Fair

What have all the Deadheads been doing since Jerry died? One thing is for sure, a lot of them are at the Oregon Country Fair every year, which has occurred every second weekend in July since the 1969 Summer of Love. Come hang with 45,000 hippies, yippies, yuppies, drippies, puppies and about everyone and everything in between and beyond at this wonderful woodsy event which takes 3,000 or so volunteers all year to plan. When you pass the seven-foot kaleidoscope at the entrance ($10 Friday and Sunday, $15 Saturday), ask about the Public Art Booth, where you can choose from an assortment of costumes or masks that will help you blend into the myriad of ongoing parades and pageants. Wander between five bandstands, four vaudeville stages, 250 craft booths and 60 food booths. In Community Village you might witness educational demonstrations, political rants and environmental pleas. Or hit Energy Park where you'll learn how to use the earth's natural energy sources in creative ways.

This colorful gathering has succeeded in preserving the counterculture balance between freedom and commitment. But leave your happy smoke and silly paper at home. The local district attorney has come down hard on the drug trafficking that generally occurs and, as Oregon's drug-forfeiture law states, the government has the power to seize property and bank accounts before a court hearing. So tune in and drop by, but leave the turning on behind.

For more information, call 541/343-4298 or visit www.oregoncountryfair.org.

PENNSYLVANIA

PENNSYLVANIA

 Lahaska

Peddler's Village

This place is tourist-trap central, a glorified strip mall pushing itself as an authentic eighteenth-century village, including seventy-five curio shops and a sixty-six-room inn set on forty-two landscaped acres with winding brick walkways. Throughout the year, the "village" hosts season-oriented festivals and contests. There's the Teddy Bear Picnic every July for owners and buffs of all ages. Then there's the Scarecrow Competition and Display (September to October) and the Gingerbread House Competition and Display (November to January).

For more information, call 215/794-4000 or visit www.peddlersvillage.com.

 Millersville

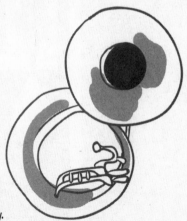

International Tuba Day

When you think of a tuba player, does the following image come to mind? Fat, pudgy-cheeked, back-of-the-line, musically talentless, personality-less bag-of-wind? If so, you have tuba issues and you just might do yourself and the world of tubists a favor and hit the annual International Tuba Day celebration held every May. The event has been held since 1982, in recognition of tubists in musical organizations around the world who have to go through the hassle of handling a tuba. What organizer Joel Day wants people to understand is that tubas are the backbone of any band. Not only is this a big feel-good support group, there's also lots of great tuba music on hand. Some fifty brass huggers show up every year to blow themselves proud. The crowd? Well, it's a whopping 300 people... but it's free.

For more information, call 717/872-3439 or visit www.joelday.com/TubaDay.

Viking Encampment

Every September during odd years, the American-Swedish Historical Museum takes festivalgoers back thousands of years. Attractions include mock sword battles, instructions in Viking shipbuilding (which can be useful if you fear the Second Flooding), cooking demonstrations, plus educational classes for children in rune-stone rubbing and how to read the runic alphabet—you know, useful stuff.

For more information, call 215/389-1776.

◄ Stahlstown

Flax Scutching Festival

In the early 1700s there were no Gap khakis and no Old Navy fleece jackets. Back then folks mostly made their own clothes. But today, flax scutching, or the art of creating linen from the flax plant, has been all but lost. Thanks to Stahlstown, which since 1907 has been taking people back to a simpler time with their Flax Scutching Festival, held every September, the art of spending three days to make one shirt is coming back. The funny thing here is that it's not the oldest flax-scutching event in the nation. It's the second oldest. Oh, what it must feel like to be number two in the flax-scutching world. But don't let that fact keep you away. There's lots of outdated fun for the whole family: wheat weaving, carving apple-headed dolls, quilting, leather crafting, gospel, outdoor worship and a mock Indian raid. This is a free event.

For more information, call 724/593-2119.

RHODE ISLAND

National Scrabble Championship

his is Rhode Island's single lame-ass entry. No, it's not the World Scrabble Championship, which will be held in 2001 in New York City, this is just the National Scrabble Championship, and it's not even a regular gig. The nationals and the world events swap years and always change locations. But for die-hard Scrabblers, it doesn't matter where the event is held, just as long as they get to use those U-less Q words, vicious vowel dumps and two-letter teasers. Close to 600 men and women over the age of twenty pay $75 to enter this barn burner held every November.

For more information, call 516/477-0033 or visit www.scrabble-assoc.com.

AMERICA BIZARRO

SOUTH CAROLINA
SOUTH DAKOTA

SOUTH CAROLINA

Aiken

Lobster Races

Don't miss the annual Lobster Races that take place in Aiken during the month of May.

For details call 803/641-1111.

Camden

Fire Fest

The small town of Camden has a history that's burning to be told. Let's see, there was the fire of 1781 (which leveled the town), the fire of 1812, the fire of 1829, the fire of 1879 … You get the picture. It only seems right that they host the annual Fire Festival, which is held every September and geared toward celebrating the work of their local fireman, who have been busy over the years. Come see an old-fashioned fire muster, upwards of fifty modern and antique fire engines, plus the proverbial bucket-brigade competition. It's all free!

For further information, call 803/432-9841.

Tripoli International High-Power Rocket Launch

If you've seen the movie *October Sky*, you already have a good feel for what this annual LDRS (Large and Dangerous Rocket Ships) gathering is all about. In fact, Quentin Wilson, one of the four boys portrayed in the movie, showed up at the 1999 gathering to give his nod of approval. This is the largest and most prestigious launching of rockets in America, held annually in July in various places around the nation. (In 2001 it will occur at Gerlach, Nevada.)

To call these rockets toys is an extreme understatement. Some stand 30 feet tall and are equipped with the same solid rocket fuel the space shuttle uses, which propels them to altitudes of 30,000 feet. Event organizer and launcher Bruce Lee says, "Someday soon, probably in the next year, one of us is going to send a rocket into outer space." (Launchers consider fifty miles up to be outer space.) "Imagine," he says, "being the first nongovernmental body to leave the atmosphere." But this event isn't just for the big boys. Rocket launchers—over 400 in all—from every class are welcome. The annual registration fee is $35 for launching, but if you aim to be one of the one hundred-plus spectators, the event is free.

For more information, call 801/225-9306 or visit www.tripoli.org.

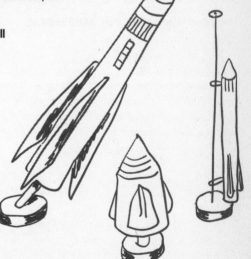

Chitlin' Strut

Chitlin', chitlings, chitterlings, they are all the same—more than three feet of hog intestine, boiled until tender, then battered and deep fried. Since 1965 the small town of Salley (population 495) has hosted the strut, a weekend honoring the chitlin', one of the deep South's most time-honored delicacies. Some folks say this dish is an acquired taste with a unique flavor somewhere between beef tripe and cow belly. And the smell, it's similar to a maggot-infested possum that's been sitting on the side of the highway for about six days. "They're pretty bad smelling," says Town Clerk Peggy Yon. "Some people say the smell sends even the flies packing. But if you put some good hot sauce on the fried chitlin', you can barely even taste it going down."

Can you believe anyone actually eats these things? Excuse me, sir, how much for the feces kabob? I mean, come on. Yet Salley's strut attracts some 40,000 gut-gorgers every November, who put away about 10,000 pounds of chitlins. (South Carolina's own Strom Thurmond shows up every year.) Beware, hour-long lines for $7 plates of chitlins, slaw and Wonder Bread can leave you feeling like a limp pickle. But once you get your food, you can relax under a shady tree to the sights and sounds of the annual Strut (dance) and Hawg-Calling contests. While entrance to the Chitlin' Strut is free, $1 donations are kindly accepted.

For more information, call 803/258-3485.

SOUTH DAKOTA

Gary

Wild Game Cookoff

If you've killed something edible, which can be just about anything in small-town South Dakota, and you have a pot big enough to cook it in, you're game for this July event. The categories are porridge and roasted meat. Mmmm, good! But that's not all contestants are judged on. Each chef must tell a whopper about how he or she caught the critter cooking in the pot. Fun for the whole family.

For more information, call 605/874-2940.

Corn Palace Festival

Mitchell's claim to fame? It is the home of the world's only Corn Palace. The original palace was more like a shack. Erected in 1892, it was called the Corn Belt Exposition. An organic structure, it was the place where successful farmers would come with their fruits, grains and vegetables, which were then attached to the exterior of the building, thus proving the fertility of South Dakota soil. But the local government soon decided that it wasn't safe for people to congregate in such a flimsy building and began planning a new venue.

The present Corn Palace, which now towers above Mitchell, wasn't erected until 1921, but it still shows off the cream of the South Dakota crops. And in this part of South Dakota, corn is king. At this annual August festival, locals celebrate the harvest by redecorating the Corn Palace. Over 275,000 ears of corn are used every year to make thirteen large murals on the outside walls of the building. For every festival, there's a new theme, 2000's being "www.millennium.corn," which will celebrate scenes from the millennium, such as "The Rock 'n' Roll Era," "The Depression Era," "World War II" and others. This event draws 20,000 visitors, who also come for the food, music and carnival. This is a free event.

For more information, call 605/995-8420 or visit www.cornpalace.org.

Sturgis Motorcycle Rally and Races

The biggest bike rally of them all, Sturgis, in recent years has found mainstream appeal. Well, sort of, if you're the type of person who can stand tall or ride mean in a small town in South Dakota's Black Hills, where 375,000 bikers come to get really wasted, fight and leave skid marks all over your face. It's really not so bad, but still, no matter how many cops patrol the perimeter, it's still hard to teach old dogs with ponytails, beer guts and tattoos new tricks. One thing for sure is that the Sturgis rally has been the motorcycle maniac's dream since its rough-and-tumble debut in 1940.

Besides the sea of Harleys parked everywhere (knock one down and you're as good as stew), this annual August event promises high-speed drag races, motorcycle rides for the kids, showcases of new products and various bike exhibits like the Rat's Hole Chopper Show, not to mention the permanent collection at the National Motorcycle Museum. Then there's some good old-fashioned entertainment for adults like lots of booze and the Lady's World Championship Pickle Lickin' Contest. Don't ask. But bet your gas money that come nightfall the bare boobs abound. And if you get tired of all the mayhem, enjoy some of the best scenery imaginable, from the Badlands to Mount Rushmore to Devils Tower, they're all just a short scoot away.

For more information, call 605/347-6570 or visit www.rally.sturgis.sd.us.

Polkafest

Polka, a folk dance that originated in Bohemia in the 1830s, is gearing up to take America by storm. Dare I say that polka just might be the next Swing? The centerpiece of Gap commercials? Bands like the Coppersmiths becoming as household as Louis Prima? Chuck Stastny, one of polka music's biggest supporters, and lots of other obscure polka bands with horrible names like Karl and the Country Dutchmen are banking on it. July 15, 2000, marks the first ever Polkafest in Tabor. It's sponsored by Stastny, America's foremost polka-music authority, whose radio show "Chuck Stastny's Top Ten Polka Music Countdown" can be heard on radio stations around the country. This annual two-day gathering expects at least 1,000 people, who will come to listen and dance to some of the hottest polka in the nation. Fees will be $12 for adults. Children under sixteen who are accompanied by an adult will be admitted for free.

For more information, call 605/668-0935 or visit www.polkacountdown.com.

TENNESSEE
TEXAS

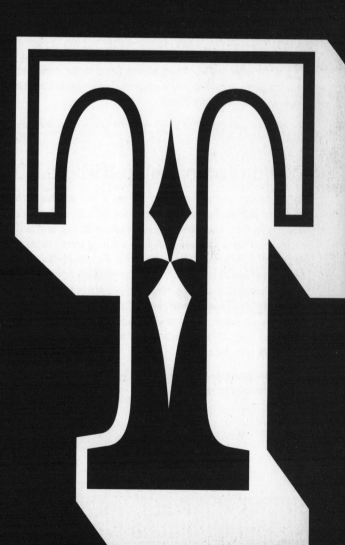

TENNESSEE

Elvis Week

Every August, Graceland hosts Elvis Week, a tribute to the all-around legacy of this larger-than-life American icon. Come for the music and the camaraderie experienced by pork-chop-sporting, jumpsuited impersonators from all over the world, who pack in by the droves.

For details call 800/238-2000 or visit www.elvis-presley.com.

World Championship Barbecue Contest

On the banks of the Big Muddy, the city of Memphis has hosted the World Championship Barbecue Contest since 1977. It's such a big deal that over fifty cities and towns across the United States hold their own sanctioned barbecue cook-offs in hopes that their local hero will bring home the bone. Memphis in May, which is the name of the finger-licking, three-day festival that surrounds the contest, annually attracts about 90,000 pork-picking Americans, who pay $6 for the daily pleasure of watching over 250 big-bellied contestants baste, grill, smoke and generally just ham it up for the title of top hog. Over thirty tons of pork are cooked, which judges rate in three different categories: whole hog, shoulder and ribs. Other competitions include those for the best barbecue sauce and the hottest chicken wings.

For more information, call 901/525-4611 or visit www.memphisinmay.com.

Dollywood Harvest Festival

When I started this collection, I told myself I wouldn't include theme-park events, but Dollywood is so odd that I had to make mention of their largest event of the year, the Harvest Festival, held over the entire month of October. But first, what the hell is Dollywood? It's a theme park in the Great Smoky Mountains, which opened in 1986. The theme? You guessed it, everything that is, was and ever will be Dolly Parton. Think Six Flags with a hillbilly twist. There are lots of rides, like the Tennessee Tornado, which is the world's first spiral-loop roller coaster. And then there's Thunder Road, the world's largest turbo-ride action adventure, which takes you on a high-speed Tennessee moonshine chase with federal agents. Head back in time as you learn the mountain way of making lye soap, the art of cooperage (barrel making) and enjoy a demonstration on how to call wild animals from Ted Peters, who took first place in a recent U.S. Open National Turkey Call Championships. There's a grist mill on the premises, Uncle Dan's Broom Shop, a pork-rind stand and the Ham 'n' Beans restaurant. During the Harvest Festival you can expect to see an antique RV collection, plus the Southern Gospel Jubilee, which is the country's largest celebration of Southern Gospel Music. One-day admission to the park is always $29.99 for adults, $24.99 for seniors, and $20.99 for the kids.

For more information, call 423/428-9486 or visit www.dollywood.com.

TEXAS

Austin

Spamarama

Not many American cities contain the perfect measure of eccentricity and redneck needed to pull off an event based around Spam. But Austin does, and locals Dick Terry and David Arnsburger have been pulling it off in style since 1978 at this annual pandemonius potted-pork party. Their idea sizzled out of a conversation about the Texas tradition of barbecue and chili cook-offs. Believing that traditional cook-offs were easy, Dick remarked that real cooks should be measured by whether of not they can make Spam taste good. Hence, the Spam-Off was born. Other events include the Spam Toss, the Spam Burger–Eating Contest and, the newest of the bunch, the Pork Pull. This is a tug-of-war event, in which each team tries to pull the other into a pool of Spam jelly. Spamarama now attracts almost 10,000 people every May. Price for entry is $5.

For more information, call 512/834-1960 or visit www.spamarama.com.

O. Henry Pun-off World Championships

A pun is a play on words, either on different senses of the same word or on similar senses and sounds of different words. Here and there they can be rather amusing, but take the joke to the extreme and it can be downright pun-ishing. Case in point is the O. Henry Pun-off World Championships, held every May in the backyard of the O. Henry Museum, located in the heart of downtown Austin. Since 1977, would-be word butchers from around the world have been ensuring that this carnival of corn is one of the punniest shows on earth. See what I mean?

Francis McGrath got into puns quite by accident. In 1991, she was still in college, a University of Texas senior, sick in bed the week before her final exams. "I turned on the TV and found the Pun-off from the year before," she says. "I don't know if it was the Pun-off or the fever, but I thought it was one of the funniest things I ever saw." It took phonetic Francis six more years to gain the gumption to enter, so, in 1997, she competed in a High Lies & Low Puns match, which pitted her against a former champion. The topic was big business. "My best was, 'Did you hear they are minting a new one-cent piece with the image of Jesus Christ on it? It's called the J.C. Penney." Sadly, with doozies like that, she didn't win. But in 1998, she came up with a great idea for the Punniest of Show competition, which is a ninety-second freestyle event. What did Francis do? The week before the show, she wrote a medley of songs, one for each letter of the alphabet. Some of the best include: "Let it B ... Oh, say can you C ... H she sweet ... K sera, sera ... Another reason for making woop-P ... V-va Las Vegas ..." you get the drift. While Francis is having a hell of a lot of pun, she says, "I try to keep it under control. Most punners keep a notebook by their beds. I'm not typical for the event, but I do pick a topic and practice occasionally to myself when I'm on the bus. I might pick a topic like cars and try to dodge distractions, ford gaps in my thinking and practice tirelessly."

For more information, call 512/472-1903 or visit www.ci.austin.tx.us/parks/ohenry.htm.

World Championship BBQ Goat Cook-off

Yep, it's just what it sounds like. Every Labor Day Weekend since 1973, Brady has hosted an event for lovers of BBQ goat. These days, the event attracts upwards of 15,000 curious folks. While the event is free, to compete you'll have to provide all your own equipment and shell out a $150 registration fee. If you're not entering, the only thing you have to pay for is your fill of goat. Other attractions include country favorites such as horseshoes, washers, plus a cowboy church service.

For more information, call 915/597-9648.

Bryan

StompOff

Wine is fine, roses I can take in doses, but a StompOff...now that's a friggin' party! Come to this annual festival held at the Messina Hof Winery & Resort every April and cheer on teams of grape stompers who compete to become the Grape-Stomping Champions of the Western World. Or shed your shoes and try to fill a 750 milliliter-bottle faster than the pros. If your experience with grape stomping is little to nil, just get in there and creatively stomp (maybe to the tune of "I Can't Drive 55") your way to the form title. Don't worry, Messina Hof does not use these grapes in their wine.

For more information, call 409/778-9463 or visit www.messinahof.com.

Great Texas Mosquito Festival

In the moist and muggy southwestern part of Texas sits the small town of Clute. To honor their healthy population of mosquitoes, every July they throw a three-day festival. Begun in 1980, this event now attracts almost 25,000 people. While there's just about everything you might expect at a small town festival— food, beer, rides and games—some of the contests deserve special mention. There's the Mosquito Legs Contest, where men and women are judged by how skinny their legs are, and then there's the Mosquito-Calling Contest, where people are judged by their creative interpretations of a mosquito call. Looking over the entire event
is Willie Man Chew, the world's largest mosquito, a twenty-five-foot tall Texas mosquito decked out in a cowboy hat and boots.

For more information, call 800/371-2971.

Texas Aggie Bonfire

At Texas A&M University, the biggest annual event is the Aggie football game versus their rivals, the University of Texas Longhorns. To celebrate the occasion, they build the biggest log bonfire in the nation, a tradition that dates back to 1909. This event made news in 1999 after toppling and killing twelve of the fifty-odd students climbing the stack. At press time, it was undetermined whether or not the burn would continue, though it seems highly probable.

Months before the November burn date, some 5,000 students cut hundreds of trees from land donated by owners who need their land cleared, which amounts to the biggest annual waste of trees in America. It takes thousands of man hours, lots of muscle, not to mention the help of a crane to erect the monster in seven levels—what they call "stacks." Though Texas A&M set the world bonfire record with their 109-foot-10-inch tower in 1969, university officials, for safety reasons, now limit its height to 55 feet.

Travis Johnson is a Senior Red Pot, a title given to those who plan, construct and clean up after the event. While Red Pots are plagued all year-round by organizing the nitty-gritty details, the honor of adding an outhouse to the top of the log pyramid is reserved for them. The outhouse is painted orange and reads "TU Frathouse." Red Pots also get to light the fire. Johnson says, "We use a mixture of gas and diesel, and it's sprayed on by the hundreds of gallons by a firetruck. Then we get to throw the torches. It lights up pretty fast."

It goes without saying that liquored-up Longhorns have attempted to sabotage the bonfire many times throughout its long history. Some of the more creative attempts happened in 1933 and 1948, when they tried to ignite the bonfire early by dropping firebombs from planes. In 1956, they even tried explosives. But the only people

EVEN THE CAMPFIRES ARE BIG IN TEXAS

TEXAS AGGIE BONFIRE
1998

© 1998 Meeks / Svatek

MEEKS/SVATEK

ever successful at tumbling the stack before the bonfire's lighted has been the Aggies themselves. Go figure. In 1994, just a week before the burning, the entire stack fell like Lincoln Logs.

The burning itself is mayhem, a drunkfest to say the least. But long after the party has ended, the bonfire continues to burn and smolder. Many of the students return once it has cooled to collect a memory. Johnson says, "Three weeks later I went to collect some ashes from the burn site, but it was still so hot it melted my spoon." Then Johnson tells me about his father, who was part of the crew who erected the world-record stack in 1969. "When he came back from Christmas break, that thing was still burning. The whole thing and the history are incredible."

For more information, call 800/777-8292 or visit www.bonfire.tamu.edu.

Hogeye Festival

Cows may be kings in Texas, but hogs are . . . fat, dirty, weird creatures that taste good with eggs. And to celebrate their importance to the economy of itty-bitty Elgin, since 1987 the town has been hosting the Hogeye Festival every October. Come ham it up chasing a greased pig, test your hog-calling technique and register for a chance to win $1,500 playing cow-patty bingo.

For more information, call 512/281-5724 or visit www.elgintx.com.

Chisholm Trail Round-up Festival

The annual Chisholm Trail Round-up Festival every June is a Western-themed event that includes mock gunfighting, plus Pig and Armadillo Races.

For details call 817/625-7005.

American Institute of Architects Sandcastle Competition

Leave it to nutty over-achieving architects to come up with the largest and most competitive sand castle contest in the nation. Since 1986 Texas architects have been descending upon Galveston's East Beach every June to sink their toes in the sand and begin building. But don't expect plastic shovels and day-glow buckets. With an annual audience of about 20,000, these hardcore beach bums are out for some serious blood. In 1999 2,200 competitors on seventy-five teams each transformed a ten-by-ten-foot plot of sand into a high-rise work of art in a matter of five hours. "The competition has gotten pretty fierce," says event spokesperson Martha Murphree. "Blueprints and all. And now most teams are equipped with landscape architects and contractors who have earth movers and mechanized water pumps." When all is said and done, team members and their creations are judged on originality of concept, artistic execution, technical difficulty, carving technique and utilization of site. Ancillary awards, such as Most Hilarious, Most Lifelike and Crowd Favorite, are also given out. Although the event is free, parking is $5.

For more information, call 713/520-0155 or visit www.aiasandcastle.com.

Art Car Parade

Although a rival of California's ArtCar Fest (see page 26), Houston's gathering celebrates paradeable art, rather than useful art—a difference the California men and women insist be made. Part of the Houston International Festival, the city's biggest celebration of the arts, the Art Car Parade is the nation's oldest (since 1987) and largest Art Car gathering, which is sponsored by the Orange Show Foundation and Pennzoil. After the parade, name judges—artists and car collectors themselves (Dusty Hill from ZZ Top, for instance)—give out all kinds of awards and prizes: Best Classic Car, Best Contraption (chariots, couches, lawn mowers, wheelchairs), Best Low Rider, Best Political Statement and many others. The winner of the People's Choice award goes home with $1,500. The total cash award in all categories is $9,800. While the parade, held in April, costs nothing to watch, there is an $18 entry fee for all you aspiring art-car artists. Applications are available on-line.

For more information, call 713/926-6368 or visit www.orangeshow.org.

World Future Society Conference

The World Future Society is the leading organization devoted to helping humans deal with the ominous weight of the future. About 1,000 people ranging from scholars to scientists to tech-heads to just ordinary folk participate in organized discussions and workshops. The goal is to grapple with important issues that face everyone in the near future. There are sessions of interest to everyone, from business to education to new technologies to social change to economics. This is an annual, roaming conference that usually takes place during the last week of July. The location is Houston for 2000 and Minneapolis for 2001.

For more information, call 800/989-8274 or visit www.wfs.org.

King Ranch

Kingsville is the town named after Texas's pride and joy, the King Ranch, the oldest and largest working ranch in history. Experience real ranch life at the South Texas Ranching Heritage Festival held every February.

For details call 800/333-5032.

Longview

Hands on a Hard Body

Made famous by S.R. Bindler's uproariously funny documentary film by the same name, Hands on a Hard Body is a contest of epic proportions. Each year since 1992, twenty-four contestants have been chosen out of a hopper at Joe Mallard Nissan in Longview. Individuals attempt to outlast the competition by standing under the hot September sun with one hand on the body of a brand new Nissan Frontier truck, without leaning. The record is ninety-two hours and forty minutes. That's just three hours and twenty minutes short of four days! While there's a five-minute break every hour and a fifteen-minute break every six hours, the contest is still a veritable mega-marathon, where physical strength, mental stability, diet and choice of footwear are major factors. As the 1994 winner Benny Perkins says in the film: "If you can't hunt with the big dogs, you get up on the porch with the puppies."

Philip Calhoun is the 1998 winner, the man who holds the record. "I stumbled up on the contest," he says. "My neighbor done it. And I'm telling you, once you get around it you kind of get attached to it." Calhoun came in second in 1993, though he didn't win a used truck, because that was before it was offered to the runner-up. "I learned from my mistakes the first go-round," he says. To prepare for the 1998 contest, Calhoun admits to jogging and working out like a man possessed. Knowing how easy the mind can go, he did lots of research. "I started looking up stuff on the brain, on how to mentally prepare and what vitamins keep you clear-headed." His diet, he decided, would consist of eating tuna fish every hour and rice now and then for a carb boost. "Tuna is pure protein," he says. "I knew that way I wouldn't have any waste in my system."

But no matter how hard you prepare, nothing can keep your blood pressure from rising and your ankles from swelling. To battle the pain in his ankles, Calhoun wore a pair of tight panty hose and took lots of Tylenol 3. But probably the biggest obstacle is the mind. "You get to a point where you forget what you're doing," Calhoun says. "And you hang on by people just telling you what to do." This is where a good cheering section becomes vital. Calhoun told his family and friends that he could handle the first several days, but for the last two he would have to depend on their direction.

As the mind goes the hallucinations come. And they come in waves—some at fifty hours, some at eighty and so forth. One recent participant claimed to be working on his truck, another claimed to be pulling his girlfriend whose hair was caught in a fan. "When the last person before me dropped out," Calhoun says, "everybody had to come over and tell me it was over. And there I was thinking we was filming a movie." Then comes recovery. Calhoun's ankles remained black-and-blue for weeks. For two to three months afterward, Calhoun says, "I'd wake up in the morning with my hands on my bed, thinking I couldn't go to the bathroom until I heard the whistle."

For more information, call 903/758-4135.

Hushpuppy Olympics

If you think a hushpuppy is a type of squishy shoe, you might as well skip this entry, city loser. Since that probably didn't scare you away, I'll tell you this one thing before you have to skip to another page: Hushpuppies are Southern folks' answers to bonbons. If you really want to know how important hushpuppies are in these parts, just ask any little girl what dances around in her head at Christmas. No, not pussy sugar-plums, try crispy little nuggets of deep-fried corn bread. I'm telling you, they flit around in Southern minds like fat little fairies. At Easter, we don't even hunt eggs, we pig...okay, you get the picture. And since you're already halfway through this, you might as well read on...pansy.

Every September since 1972, little Lufkin, Texas, has paid humble homage to these mini–golden globes. Part of the Texas State Forest Festival, contestants from around the state compete for the well-worshipped crown. And hey, anyone can enter. All you have to do is bring your cooking gear, because the good people at Brookshire Brothers/HYTOP provide all the corn and oil any good gut grenade needs. All you need to bring is your special fictions. You want to make the first peanut butter and jelly hushpuppy, well go right ahead. Trout and cauliflower? Corned-beef hash and spinach?

Whatever your pleasure, just step up to the plate. But know this: Your ideas are disgusting. Conform, you bastard. Pack that bitch with a little fresh corn, cheddar, jalapeños and beer. Then maybe, just maybe, you might have a shot at winning. What do you win? Cash money, honey. Good old American green. And if you can't cook worth a toot in a vacuum, there's a showmanship competition that gives every boob a chance to shine. Come one, come all.

For more information, call 409/634-6305.

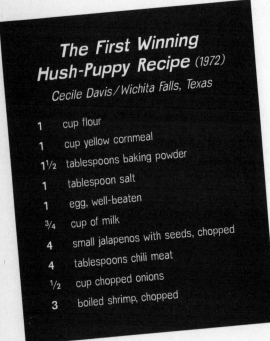

The First Winning Hush-Puppy Recipe (1972)

Cecile Davis / Wichita Falls, Texas

1	cup flour
1	cup yellow cornmeal
1½	tablespoons baking powder
1	tablespoon salt
1	egg, well-beaten
¾	cup of milk
4	small jalapenos with seeds, chopped
4	tablespoons chili meat
½	cup chopped onions
3	boiled shrimp, chopped

World Championship
Watermelon Seed Spit

Luling is a 5,000-person town plum full of melon heads—watermelon wackos in love with Royal Sweets, Jubilees, and Yellow Dollies, to name a few. As a tip of the hat to their agricultural godsend and to the farmers themselves, Lulingians have been hosting the annual Watermelon Thump every June since 1954. Now almost 35,000 people show up every year for all sorts of watermelon-related activities, including eating and carving competitions. There is also a contest for the largest watermelon grown that year, the record being eighty-one pounds back in 1962. Each year, the record watermelon is sent to celebrities like Art Linkletter, Johnny Carson and Ronald Reagan. In 1999 they added the watermelon-carving contest. The only rule is that you must be able to wear whatever you carve on your head like a hat.

However, the biggest draw—due to lots of national television publicity—is the seed-spitting championship. Hawkers of all ages line up for a chance to beat *The Guinness Book of World Records* and take home $1,000. The standing record is 68 feet and 9.125 inches set by Luling-local Lee Wheells in 1989. If you think this is all for fun, you are dead wrong, mister. Watermelon spitting in Luling is serious business. There are official seed-spitting songs and yells: "Come on everybody, take a look, [insert name] gonna spit into the record book ..." The competition is fierce and the rules are followed religiously. Contestants are docked for spitting in the crowd, and any person caught using nonsanctioned, illegal seeds will be disqualified.

For more information, call 830/875-3214 or visit www.bcsnet.net/lulingcc.

World's Largest Rattlesnake Round Up

ate snakes? "Well, this ain't no place you'd be interested in," says Laverl Stephens, world-renowned snake handler. Just as he does every second weekend in March, this year Laverl will be showing off his technique to about 30,000 fang-fearing folks at the World's Largest Rattlesnake Round Up in Sweetwater. Since 1958, local Jaycees (town do-gooders) have organized ranchers and farmers into thinning out their pesky population of Western diamondback rattlesnakes. Why? They present a threat to livestock. "You see," Laverl says, "that old rattlesnake, he'll coil on up there to sleep. And that old cow—they get a little curious sometimes—will go on up there and stick they nose right on down and the snake will hit him and they head'll swell on up real big and they'll suffocate."

Since its inception, over 225,000 pounds of the restless rattlers have been rounded. "The way you do it is you get yourself one of them weed sprayers and fill it with gas, and you spray the fumes down in those dens. Then you just trap'em up in a bag and bring'em to us. We take live snakes only." Although the biggest snake in the round-up's history was just over fifteen pounds and pushing six feet in length, the average weight borders two singles. They are expecting somewhere in the ballpark of three tons total this year. That's a lot of hissing honeys, which, bottom line, translates into a lot of cold, hard cash for the town of Sweetwater.

Before the event, the Jaycees take bids from buyers for the skins, the meat and the venom. The skins are used to make boots, rock-star digs and everything in between. The meat is considered a delicacy both at home and abroad (meaning Oklahoma). And the venom is used for medicinal purposes. Having accepted their green, the Jaycees pay everyone who hauls in a sack of slitherers an average of about $4 per pound. "One year a while back," Laverl says, "the price got up to $8.50 a pound. Everybody was out hunting. There was grandmas and grandpas doing it. People was having to guard their snakes so nobody else stole 'em." Talk about getting snaked.

The weekend is packed with all sorts of family events. There's the Miss Snake Charmer Contest, rattlesnake dances, snake-handling demonstrations, guided snake hunts, plus a host of other things you'd find at your everyday ordinary backyard rattlesnake-slaughter fest, including lessons in skinning and grilling and, of course, snake milking (the process of extracting the venom from the snake). A lesson in milking: Hand gripped snug behind the head of the snake, you hang its fangs over the lip of a glass jar and squeeze the venom sacks, which are right behind its eyes. "Usually with them big snakes," Laverl says, "you have to use both hands on the head, so you throw the other end between your legs and hold on."

THE PRE-SLAUGHTER SNAKE PIT

LAVERL STEVENS

As you can imagine, no reptile-decimating carnival of such colossal proportions is without its opponents. "Some of them protesters come every year," says Laverl. "One guy even dresses up like a grim reaper." While the Jaycees stand firm on the notion that they aren't doing anything to destroy the species, John "Jo Herp" Hollister, a well-known Texas snake scholar, says, "Killing large quantities of any species upsets the balance which nature has spent eons creating." Because of the decrease in the snake populations, Hollister says, "People are bringing in snakes from hundreds of miles away, often from other states."

T. Dean McInturff, President of the West Texas Herpetological Society, calls round-ups "circus sideshows" and "public butcherings." His beef is consistent with Hollister's. The primary reason is that rattlesnakes are endangered in fifteen states. Also, spraying gasoline into dens kills many other species of animals and makes the dens uninhabitable for many years, not to mention that their venom milking is a bogus front. Hollister says, "I have seen them milking three or four different species into the same container, which is left out at room temperature for hours. No respectable lab would buy that."

McInturff puts the whole shebang into perspective. "How would the public react to a Puppy Round-up, where the dogs are gassed from their dog houses, stacked in trash cans and at the end of three days beheaded and skinned? And what if little snarling puppy heads encased in glass were sold to people who enjoyed eating savory, gasoline-tainted fried-puppy meat?" Mmm . . . finger lickin' Fido.

For more information, call (915) 235-5488 or visit camalott.com/~sweetwater/rattrrup.html

UTAH

Salt Lake City

Swiss Singing and Yodeling Festival

Can you believe there are 1,000 Americans who consider themselves professional Swiss singers and yodelers? How about 5,000 spectators who care? Well, it's the truth, my friend. They all gather every June in Salt Lake City. Badges for the four-day festival run $185, but tickets for the concerts only cost between $17.50 and $27.50.

For more information, call 801/583-7091 or visit www.netessence.com/swissfest99.

Snowbird

Belly Dance Festival

Yasamina Roque is the undisputed belly-dancing queen of Utah. She and her husband Jason have been entrenched in Middle Eastern culture and *danse orientale* for over thirty years. Besides running a boutique and dance studio in Salt Lake City, since 1980 the Roques (now with their new daughter Ariana) have been organizing the oldest and largest gathering of belly dancing diehards in the nation. Over 400 performers make and appearance at this annual August event, including such mega-hit belly-dance stars as Judeen, Joynan, Dahlal, Aziz and everybody's favorite, the lovely Jawahare. While the shows are free for the 15,000-plus crowd that shows every year, seminars with the featured artists run about $30 a pop, which is nothing compared to the thrill of learning, say veil technique from delicious Delilah, the art of Egyptian cabaret from Sahra, or choreography from the FatChanceBellyDance troupe.

For more information, call 801/486-7780 or visit www.aros.net/~kismet.

World Senior Games

Every year in October since 1989, local philanthropist Jon M. Huntsman has sponsored the World Senior Games. Billed as "the premier sporting event for seniors," contestants must be fifty years of age or older. Warning: Unless you want a right hook to the kisser, don't call a fifty-year-old man or woman a senior anywhere else but in St. George. Upwards of 5,000 gray-bound athletes show up every year to compete in sports such as basketball, tennis, cycling, golf, horseshoes, racquetball, softball and volleyball. There are a total of nineteen sporting events to compete in, plus health screenings for men and women, which include free PSA testing, mammograms and cholesterol and glaucoma readings. Registration for this weeklong event is just $59.

For more information, call 800/562-1268 or visit www.seniorgames.net.

VERMONT
VIRGINIA

VERMONT

International Rotten Sneaker Contest

Did you know that each foot contains 250,000 sweat glands that can produce up to a pint of sweat per day? That was the impetus behind Odor-Eaters products, sponsors since 1988 of the International Rotten Sneaker Contest, held every March in Montpelier. The rotten-sneak craze is catching on. Kids ranging in age from five to fifteen compete in regional contests all over the world—from Alaska to Italy. The regional champs bring their most stinky, worn-out, frayed and torn tennies to Vermont to compete for a $500 U.S. Savings Bond and a year's supply of Odor-Eaters. Probably the biggest award for winners is that their rotten sneakers will be enshrined in the Hall of Fumes, further securing their place in rotten-sneaker history.

For more information, call 212/371-2200.

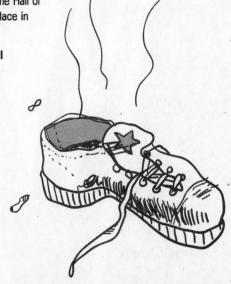

VIRGINIA

Old Fiddlers Convention

There's no better place than a small town in the Blue Ridge Mountains to kick back and enjoy some of the hottest fiddle players in the country. Held every August since 1935, this event attracts about 50,000 fiddle enthusiasts of every ilk, who come to see some 2,000 musicians compete in categories like old-time fiddle, Dobro, mandolin, Autoharp, dulcimer, bluegrass banjo and many others. Some well-known names include: Jimmy Martin, Ronnie Bowman, Sammy Shelor and Junior Sisk, just to name a few.

Better than the staged contests are the impromptu jam sessions that fire up in the campground area, which is packed with RVs and hippie-like vans. If you've been to a Grateful Dead show, this parking lot scene is similar. While you won't hear acid vendors hawking doses, smelling the sweet aroma of marijuana is a given. And no mountain music festival of such epic proportions is complete without some serious clogging and flat-foot dancing, which tends to go on late into the night, every night. Entrance to the convention grounds runs between $5 and $8 for this four-day fiddling extravaganza. Camping spots, which fill up fast, go for $60.

For more information, call 540/236-8541 or visit www.ls.net/~stever/fiddlers.html.

Slug Festival

ere's some slug trivia for you. Slugs have been around since the dinosaurs. The wet Olympic coast is home to twenty-three species of slugs. They have two tentacles, one for seeing and the other for feeling. Because their tentacles movie independently, they can see in two directions at once. Slugs have 27,000 teeth and eat their weight every day. It would take more than nine hours for a slug to finish a hundred-yard dash: That's why the organizers of the annual Slug Festival, held every July, no longer hold slug races. "It just wasn't much fun," Susan Hulbert of the Northwest Trek Wildlife Park says. So, instead of racing slugs, they gather up several different species from the forest and put them on display. The slug native to this area of Washington is the banana slug, which is green and yellow and can be the length of a banana, too. In addition to educational talks about these mini mollusks, there's lots of slimy games for the kids.

For more information, call 360/832-7152 or visit www.nwtrek.org.

Langley

Mystery Weekend

very February since 1984, the Whidbey Island village of Langley, a small artists' colony outside Seattle, transforms its three-by-two-block row of shops and B&Bs into a stage worthy of Broadway. Get out your best Sherlock Holmes cap and pipe, because every third weekend of that month a murderous mystery is staged by a number of its 1,050 local residents—town barber, banker, mechanic, et cetera—and set for solving by the 800 to 1,200 visitors in attendance every year. All would-be crime-stoppers need to sign up at the Langley Visitor and Information Center at 208 Anthes Street. The price to play the two-day who-done-it is just a buck.

This is how it works. At registration you will receive *The Langley Gazette*, which has the fictitious crime outlined in news articles. Recent headlines read: "GOLD! Lost loot lies off Langley" and "Murder silences high-C's serenade." Also in your registration packet will be a clue map showing locations where written clues can be picked up. The rest is up to you: interviewing key players, eye witnesses, families of the deceased and even shopkeepers who might have overheard a thing or two. The presentation of the solution takes place on Sunday at 5:00 p.m. Super snoops receive free dinners, weekends at local inns and signed work by local artists.

For more information, call 360/221-5676.

Combine Demolition Derby

Here's an interesting take on your ordinary cow-town smash-up. In 1988 Bill Loomis, of Loomis Truck & Tractor, came up with the idea of a Combine Demolition Derby to spice up Lind's Centennial Celebration, held every June. The local chapter of the Lions Club decided Loomis's idea was exactly the kind of quirky event that could add considerable revenue to this struggling wheat-farming community. And they were right. For the past ten years, a handful of the 462 residents of Lind have been rescuing rusty-wheat combines from farmer's fields all around the state, preparing for what has become not only the oldest, but the biggest Combine Derby in America.

After months spent souping up the engines, modifying the exteriors for safety and garishly painting the beasts, every June these recycled behemoths creep out of rotting barns and oil-slicked garages for their fifteen minutes of fame. Under the crown of the rodeo-arena lights, about eighteen combines compete annually in several single-elimination heats. Carol Kelley, who is the only female combine operator in the competition, says, "The key is to go for the tires. These things can turn on a dime, but without tires, they can't do squat." Winners of individual heats win $125, while the winner of the final round takes home $750. Admission is $7.

For more information, call 509/677-3628 or visit www.ritzcom.net/lind/derby.html.

CAROL KELLY

THE DANCE OF THE METAL GIANTS

Stampede Suicide Race

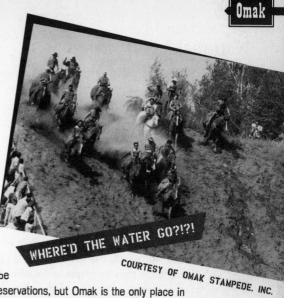

WHERE'D THE WATER GO?!?!

COURTESY OF OMAK STAMPEDE, INC.

The small town of Omak is just across the river from the Colville Indian Reservation. Since 1935 the people from both sides of the river have come together for a weekend of rodeo and extreme horse racing. The Suicide Race used to be a tradition on many local reservations, but Omak is the only place in America where it is still run. The race earns its name because about twenty riders annually drop down the steep, thirty-three degree Suicide Hill at high speed. Having survived the worst part, riders dash into the Okanogan River and then end the race in the local arena, where the rodeo is held throughout the weekend. Riders, about eighty percent of whom are Native American, train themselves and their horses year-round for this grueling competition, in which winning the $1,000 first-place prize means little compared to the amount of respect they earn for themselves and their families.

The race has received quite a bit of criticism in recent years. It's not unheard of for a horse's leg to snap or for a rider to be thrown on his or her head. Although boycotted and subsequently canceled in 1999, this is still scheduled to be an annual event that takes place every August and attracts about 8,000 people. Four races are held throughout the weekend, after the rodeo events. For a seat in the rodeo arena, you can expect to pay between $5 to $15 per day. But for the best view, buy a booster button for $3, which will give you access to the dike and a bird's-eye view of the riders plunging off Suicide Hill.

For more information, call 800/933-6625 or visit www.omakstampede.org.

National Lentil Festival

he World's Largest Bowl of Lentil Chili is served every August to honor this lovable little legume at the National Lentil Festival.

For details call 509/334-3565.

"Daffodil 200" Bed Race

t's hard to believe the annual August Puyallup bed race has only been in existence since 1985. The memories are so thick in my head, I guess it just seems like an eternity. Actually, I've never been to the race. Beds and racing just don't work for me. But it does for dozens of dreamers who compete to celebrate this great American pastime. Although a team of five can cut down the entry fee per person, it's still a whopping $200 just for a chance to win a lame-ass trophy. However, if you're up Puyallup's way and you've got cash burning a hole in your pocket, pull up a bed and get your motor running. If you don't have your own bed balanced on wheels, one can be made available—for a price, of course.

**For more information, call 253/845-6755 or visit
www.puyallupchamber.com.**

Chainsaw Carving Championships

very August since 1990 the folks who run Westport's Coho Motel have organized what has become America's largest and most respected chainsaw carving competition. About fifty professional woodsmen and power-tool hobbyists get their saws purring on huge chunks of spruce and cedar in front of a crowd of about 2,000. The only rule is that contestants must carve something with a nautical theme. The 1999 winner was a bear with a fishing pole in its mouth sitting on a salmon. Because of its pricey purse, the competition is stiff. "The winner gets $2,500, which is donated by local shops and sponsors," says Cheryl Bell, the event's accountant. At the end of the event, all of the carved pieces are auctioned off to the crowd.

For more information, call 800/572-0177.

WEST VIRGINIA

Berkeley Springs

International Water Tasting Contest

With a rich history in water dating back to 1748, when sixteen-year-old George Washington visited the Berkeley Springs as part of Lord Fairfax's surveying crew, there's no better location than the town of Berkeley Springs for a water-tasting contest. Every February since 1990, a dozen judges made up of news media from around the country (now that's a publicity coup!) sip international waters in three categories: municipal, non-carbonated bottled and sparkling. The 1999 contest received one hundred entries. Who would have ever guessed that Romania's Harghita would be named the best non-carbonated bottled water of the year? Judges test water for clarity, smell, taste and aftertaste. "Aftertaste is probably the most important," says organizer J.W. Rone. "When I get a glass of water with a bad aftertaste, well, it just ruins the whole water experience." This annual event, just like the water, is free for the 500 folks who show up every year.

For more information, call 800/447-8797 or visit www.berkeleysprings.com/water.

Roadkill Cook-off

In West Virginia no one used to argue with the notion that there ain't nothing better than finding a fresh-killed animal on the side of the road. The dirty work already done, all folks had to do was throw that critter in a pot and get ready for some ground-roots grub. Those days are long gone, however, at least for the better part of the country. That's why every September, Marlington celebrates road-killed fare with an event, that should, well, make you barf. But hold on there, no one uses real roadkill here. The animal one cooks must be one that is commonly found dead on the side of the road (possum, beaver, raccoon, snake, deer, et cetera), but the animals must not actually come from the side of the road. That's part of the official rules. Does anybody actually ever check? If you plan to cook, you need to bring all of your own equipment. As far as how to cook, the sky is the limit. Grilling, chilling, baking, flaking, flipping, dipping—whatever bites your ass. What will you be up against? Try Stewed Blood with Moose Balls on the Half Shell or Stir-Tired Possum with Natural Brown Maggots. Yep, competition is tough. But the winner can go away with $300, which to most who enter means they don't have to scoop up animals from the highway for the rest of the month.

For more information, call 800/336-7009.

Hick Festiva

Parsons is the place for the Hick Festiva held every year in September. This three-day-long event promises lots of axe-throwing, horse-pulling, jug-playing and backwoods babes competing in the annual Hick Beauty Contest.

For details call 304/478-2660.

WISCONSIN

International Jacks & Pick-Up Sticks Tournament

Bite-size Burlington's claim to fame is the Spinning Top Exploratory Museum. Throughout the year they sponsor several unique events. The annual tournament is held every last Sunday in February. Kids ages 6 to 106 are invited to compete. The entry fee is $2. Antique jacks and pick-up sticks are exhibited. Every April they also host Yo-Yo Days & Convention, where classes, demonstrations, auctions and trick contests abound. Entry to the convention is $25; individual classes cost $15.

For details call 414/763-3946.

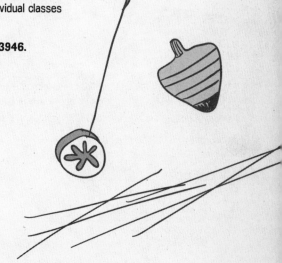

Kraut Festival

What kind of Kraut Festival would be worth a wiener without a sauerkraut-eating contest? Well, certainly not this one. Not only is this the only sauerkraut festival in America, it's the only kraut-eating contest in the world. Are you kidding? Come on you German blockheads, get with the picture! Since way back in 1950, the town of Franksville, "The Cabbage Capital of the World," has been hosting this event. Now it's an annual late-June affair that packs them in. People pay $1 a piece (or $5 a carload, for bargain shoppers) to witness people like seventeen-year old Kyle Woller put down 15.1 ounces of kraut in 42.2 seconds. He's the 1999 Champ. His technique? "Don't chew, just swallow," he says. Contestants must use a fork and the plate of kraut must remain on the table. There are three divisions of competition: Men's (two pounds/two minutes), Women's (1.5 pounds/2 minutes), Children's (1 pound/1 minute). Anyone can enter, that is anyone who doesn't mind upchucking a little kraut for the hungry crowd.

For more information, call 608/222-2899 or visit www.racine.org.

IN ONE AND OUT THE OTHER

COURTESY OF JOAN COLLINS PUBLICITY, INC.

AMERICA BIZARRO

World Championship Lumberjack Competition

ayward is a town of 2,000 with a history steeped in the logging and timber industry. It has been hosting the World Championship Lumberjack Competition during the last full weekend of July since 1958. The biggest and oldest competition of its kind in America, every year over 200 bush-bearded, barrel-chested, flannel-wearing dudes and dudettes in dungarees are invited (based on performances in smaller events around the nation) to hopefully do more than just lumber through various events.

THE NEW JENNY CRAIG DIET

BONNIE SALZMAN

In the water sports category, there's logrolling, a staple. The gist is: King of the mountain. Two people wearing spiked shoes roll a log through the water while trying to dump the other person first. The boom run is a race across swivel-attached floating logs. While the first leg is easy, navigating the swaying bunch on the return trip can be a bitch. Then there's the climbing events. Think about scurrying up ninety-foot trees, doing a little chainsaw work, then sliding back down all under the gun. Probably the big audience pleasers are the sawing and chopping events. I'm talking Popeye and Brutus on either side of a saw getting through a log with a diameter of twenty inches in 6.09 seconds. Is that even possible? Bet your ass it is. It's the world record. Another favorite is the Underhand Chop, where woodsmen and-women stand on top of an upturned log with a diameter of fourteen inches and split that mother in two with an ax. World record: 11.84 seconds.

Now, the obvious question about any sporting that involves climbing, axes and saws is how many people die every year? "None, but a guy broke his back after falling from the top of a tree," say Bonnie Salzman, event spokesperson. "We've even lost a couple of toes. These guys insist on wearing tennis shoes for the Underhand Chop. They've tried those steel-toed boots, but they saw they just can't get the traction they need." Well, one less toe never hurt anyone. But diced digits and free-flowing blood? That always gets the crowd rocking. Admission is $10 a day or $25 for the entire weekend.

For more information, call 715/634-2484.

Mustard Family Reunion

Every June since 1996, the Mount Horeb Mustard Museum has hosted a family reunion for anyone with the name Mustard or any foreign variant, such as "Senf," which is the German word for mustard. Because it's not a common name, only about one hundred Mustards from coast to coast make the journey to meet distant kin and taste each other. The Mustard Museum houses over 3,200 mustards from all over the world, plus antique mustard pots, old mustard jars, magazine ads, et cetera. "Anything having to do with mustard in history we collect," says Barry Levenson, the museum's wacky curator. Some of the best mustards on hand are medal winners from the World Mustard Competition, such as Rothchild's Raspberry-Honey Mustard or Wild Times Farms' Romano Cheese Mustard. While you might think somebody would have created a hot dog flavored mustard—you can now find hot dogs with chili in the middle—Levenson says there's no such thing. "Just a lot of herbs, fruits, whiskies, single malt scotches and wines," he says.

For more information, call 800/438-6878.

Beef-A-Rama

There's no doubt about it, inhabitants of Wisconsin go coo-coo for cow's flesh. And they are damn proud of it. Every September since 1964, residents of the small town of Minocqua have been celebrating the Almighty with a bovine bonanza fit for a . . . Texas Longhorn. But what earns the Beef-A-Rama a spot in this book is their not-so-famous Parade of Roasts. Yes, over sixty dripping roasts equaling over 1,200 pounds of mouth-watering moo-moo are paraded through the streets while silent onlookers—one hand over their hearts and one eye to heaven—stand patiently and drool. Chow-time is just around the bend. With factory-line precision, volunteers carve, slice, fold and wrap that mountain of slow-cooked flesh into thousands of sandwiches for the carnivorous crowd.

For more information, call 800/446-6784.

AirVenture

Since 1952 the Experimental Aircraft Association (EAA) has sponsored the world's largest sport aviation event. In 1999 they drew upwards of 765,000 aviation enthusiasts. Held during the last week in July every year, the event promises exhibitions of classic planes, like the only Boeing 247-D still flying, and modern planes like NASA's Flying Lab. You'll be able to learn everything you've ever wanted to learn about our first-flight pioneers at the Wright Brothers' Experience. And, of course, there are tons of air shows from some of the world's finest flying talents, including individuals like Sean Tucker and Bob Hoover, to groups like the U.S. Air Force Thunderbirds. But the biggest to-do is made of the Great Cross-Country Flying Race, a Denver to Oshkosh wing of 766 nautical miles, where the winner takes home $10,000 in gift certificates. EAA members pay $14 per day, while for non-EAA members the price is $35. There are special discounts for seniors and children.

For more information, call 920/426-4800 or visit www.airventure.org.

Burger Fest

Every first Saturday in August since 1885, the cows in the fields of Seymour, Wisconsin, get a little jumpy. It's the sight of the celebrated Outagamie County Fair, where more than a century ago, fifteen-year-old Charlie Nagreen tried hawking meatballs smothered in onions from the back of his ox-drawn cart. When his feast was less than tantalizing to fairgoers on the move, like any wild-eyed entrepreneur, Charlie imagined what has since become a worldwide institution: the American hamburger.

If the name Hamburger Charlie doesn't already ring a bell, this town of Fargo-talking folks has your name on their garage wall. Violet Guaerke, the daughter of Hamburger Charlie, says, "You know, he's not just my father. He's almost the town's father. He's the father of the hamburger." Although Vi can't remember much about anything anymore, she recalls her father's sales pitch with gusto— "Hamburger, hamburger, hamburger hot, with an onion in the middle and a pickle on top, makes your lips go flippity-flop." Although disputed by would-be hamburglars in towns like Hamburg, Pennsylvania, Athens, Texas, and Akron, Ohio, in the late eighties Seymour finally cooked its ravenous rivals after White Castle donned their referee stripes and took a national poll.

Though the world hasn't heard Hamburger Charlie's mantra in over fifty years, his legacy can be seen, if not felt in the air around Seymour. The year 1990 marked the dedication of the Hamburger Hall of Fame, a makeshift museum filled with all sorts of hamburger paraphernalia. Its most prized artifact dates back to a recent fair, when Seymour grilled *The Guinness Book of World Records*-holding hamburger, weighing in at a whoppering 5,220 pounds. Vivien Treml, President of the Home of the Hamburger, Inc., boasts, "Yeah, we built a grill the size of a two-car garage." Measuring over twenty-one feet across, the mammoth patty would have been a bitch to flip. But local steelworkers Steve Mielke and Joe Sauer had a plan. They designed a cover that had to be lifted on and off by a crane, removing the need to flip the behemoth burger. "Oh yeah," Vivien continues, "have you seen it yet? The entire grill is on display at the hamburger museum. No kidding."

This year's Burger Fest fun doesn't get started until the sun is a good three-fingers over the tree line. "My God," Vivien explains. "You should really try the Ketchup Slide. That's where people pay to slide on a mixture of ketchup and water. And we got the Bun Toss. You know, we have a local baker make a hard and heavy bun so people can throw it like a discus." Vivien goes on to leak never-before-revealed info from the halls of the Home of the Hamburger. She says that although they've had problems with stray salivating dogs, they've been lucky enough to have avoided large-beaked dive-bombing birds. She admits many locals actually eat hamburgers for breakfast in the local greasy spoons. Also, it's no doubt she's heard rumors of Ronald McDonald lurking at the outskirts of town. And it's funny, but there are no known out-of-the-closet vegetarians in Seymour. But they're looking into it. This is a free event.

For more information, call 920/833-9522.

Bratwurst Days

This is an announcement! The Bratwurst-Eating Contest at Sheboygan's annual Bratwurst Days has been discontinued. After eating 6.5 doubles (two thick and juicy brats on a roll with the works), a young man recently barfed on stage. If you want to see people safely enjoying bratwurst, this is the place. Every August.

For more information, call 920/457-9491.

Stevens Point

World's Largest Trivia Contest

Every April some 12,000 trivia buffs come to Stevens Point to compete in the World's Largest Trivia Contest. Some 530 teams, who pay $30 each to register, attempt to answer eight questions every hour for fifty-four hours. All of the questions are asked over local radio station 90FM, and contestants are given two song's lengths to come up with answers. Teams are supplied with ID and telephone numbers to use during the contest. Event organizer Oz, says, "If you think you know trivia, come to Stevens Point and play in a real trivia contest. After all the luster has worn off and you are staring at hours thirty through thirty-six knowing you have to make it through hour fifty-four, you learn that we take it very seriously." Trophies are awarded to first-, second- and third-place winners. This contest has been held since 1969.

For more information, call 715/344-8471 or visit www.easy-axcess.com/trivia.

WYOMING

Jackalope Days

For the last 150 years, the legend of the mysterious jackalope has flourished in the American West. It is said that a man from Douglas named Roy Ball, commonly referred to as "an occasionally sober trapper," first reported a sighting in 1829. The original jackalope had the body of a large jackrabbit and the horns of an antelope. They were known to reach 150 pounds. Because one has never actually been captured in the wild, not much is known about these strange and often menacing creatures. What is known is that back in the 1880s, a herd of giant jackalopes wiped out an entire settlement near Douglas and several moving wagon trains. Other sketchy information implies that they mate during lightning flashes, like to pull barbed wire off fences and love the taste of whiskey. (The practice of baiting jackalopes with whiskey has been banned as reports of drunken brawls between various furry creatures is on the rise.) Yet, the days of the huge, herculean hares has ended. Though almost totally extinct, some still report sightings of smaller, jackrabbit-sized jackalopes. We all know that most cowboys are sauceheads, but here's word from the range: Although today's jackalope is smaller than its kin of yesteryear, they are smarter and have even been known to imitate the human voice.

Every year in June, Douglas pays tribute to its unique heritage at Jackalope Days. The event is sanctioned by Wyoming Governor Ed Herschler, who has coined Douglas "Home of the Jackalope." While there are plenty hungover cowpokes on the lookout for the ever elusive jackalope that is said to show up every year and create havoc, most people just come for the good, clean fun. For the kids, there's the Mini-Monster Truck Obstacle Course; for the ladies, some serious competition at the Mud-Volleyball Tournament; for the men, a Motorcycle Show and Rally; and for the random losers, a Greased–Pig Money Run. And don't forget to get your picture next to a nine-foot statue of a jackalope, created by a local named Leonard Lore.

For more information, call 307/358-2950 or visit www.jackalope.org.

Laramie

Rocky Mountain 1000-Day

Since 1992, the U.S. Orienteering Federation has sponsored the 1000-Day, which is a weeklong orienteering festival in America. Orienteering is a sport that is rapidly catching on not only in America, but around the world. Over 600 orienteering events currently take place in America on an annual basis. So what is orienteering? It is the sport of navigating with maps and compasses to find points on the landscape. Participants set out on pre-designed courses that demand both mental and physical skills. There are different levels for participants of every ilk, men and women, young and old. Some choose the more extreme, physically challenging courses, in which they're required to sprint up mountains and across tough terrain. Some prefer to enjoy the natural settings and choose the more leisurely events. The 1000-Day occurs during the final days of July and first days of August annually. It attracts around 225 competitors every year. The cost is $100 for nine days of racing.

For more information, e-mail mikell@sprynet.com or visit www.us.orienteering.org.

INDEX

June

July

August

September